METHODS OF EXTRACTING SLATE

Slate is extracted by one of three methods. The first is 'Hillside Working'. Here it is face working where the slate is dug into the hillside to form either a single level or several. If the slate is of good quality and appears to be a continuous large vein it often becomes a quarry and is then extracted from multiple galleries or terraces. The second method is 'Pit Working'. Here a slate vein is followed down with adits or levels being driven to make life easier for transportation of the raw product. Finally there is 'Underground Working'. This occurs when there would be too much surface material to be removed. The vein is accessed by driving adits or levels. Work would then commence along the top of the vein by driving what is known as a roofing shaft. From this progress would then be downward and across to form a chamber. A typical size would be around 22 metres wide. Another chamber would then be started leaving an intervening pillar some 13 metres wide that would act as a support for the roof. Many chambers could be developed in any mine by this process.

With today's modern mining techniques a method called 'un-topping' is used to remove the surface of the ground above the vein and rob the pillars as these would be good quality slate. In its most simple form slate was extracted by attacking the slate exposure by basic and simple means such as levering and cutting out usable blocks. The tools used for this were a big oak mallet called, in Welsh a 'Rhys' and 'Plug and Feathers'. These were wedges that expanded the rock when driven into cracks.

As these workings expanded it became evident that more rock was needed so blasting took place. Initially this was black powder. Prior to mechanisation a shot hole was drilled by the use of a 'Jumpah', a long weighted iron rod. This was a very laborious slow method. After 1880 or so compressed air drills were used, much quicker but incredibly noisy. Eventually high explosives were used but this tended to shatter the rock. Only 10% of the rock extracted was usable. The usable blocks going to be used for roofing slates were then split using a chisel to a suitable thickness before being dressed to the required size. They were then held over a fixed blade, the 'Celfi' and trimmed by the use of a tool similar to a knife, 'Cyllell'.

Further developments took place with the advent of water power in the early 19th century. Circular saws developed and in the mid-20th century diamond circular saws came into use and are now universal. They are huge things having blades two metres in diameter and even slightly larger. Instead of the coarse cut of the water powered saws these saws have a very fine one but use water for cooling the blade. Having seen these work it is absolutely amazing to see a three ton block of slate over 300mm thick and 1.5 metres long sliced just as a knife goes through butter. Mechanical dressing developed around the same time as circular saws and was operated by hand or foot. However, splitting the slate still remains a manual process. Many attempts to mechanise this process failed.

WALK 1

RHOSYDD & CROESOR MINES

DESCRIPTION Apart from these two iconic mines this 6 mile walk has some grand mountain scenery. Although it does not reach any summits it is a fine circular walk with much of interest. Some route finding skills are necessary between Llyn Cwm y Foel and Llynnau Diffwys until the good path leading down to Bwlch y Rhosydd is reached. There are scenes of much dereliction around here where there was once a thriving industry. Allow 4 hours.

START From the Snowdonia National Park car park at Croesor.

DIRECTIONS Leave Porthmadog by driving past the railway station to reach a roundabout at the junction with the A487. Turn left then right at the sign for Tremadog 350 yards further to reach a 'T' junction with the A498 in Tremadog. Turn right along this and continue through Prenteg and turn right on to the B4410. Follow this and cross the Welsh Highland Railway line and past the Glasyn Osprey Project site to Garreg. Turn left on to the A4085. Continue for 400 yards and turn right at the sign for Croesor indicating 2½ miles. There are fine stone pillars here, one each side of the road! Continue along this narrow road into the village and turn left at the cross roads to the car park on the right.

1 Walk out of the car park over the footbridge and TURN RIGHT. Follow the path along an old tramway, through a kissing gate 10 yards from the bridge. Continue, noting the fine clapper bridge on the right. The path crosses an old tramway bridge to reach a gate. Go through this and continue passing through another gate to join a track. Walk straight ahead and climb over a ladder stile to the left of a gate and pass through the next gate 100 yards ahead. The track continues through a shallow cutting and up to another gate to the right of a fine slate fence.

2 Go through the gate and immediately TURN LEFT down by the side of the slate fence keeping it on the left to reach a truncated wall on the right. Go over the footbridge at the end of the wall and head towards a ruin. Walk in front of this to reach a marker post and a more pronounced path. Follow this up as it crosses the hillside diagonally to reach and climb over a ladder stile. *There are great views into Cwm Croesor from here.* Keeping the fence to the left and then a wall continue up to where this veers left. Walk straight ahead here. The path now becomes vague but quickly reappears and continues past two large boulders. When the path runs out again by the remains of a wire fence go up and left to a post. Just beyond are the remains of some slate pillars. A series of small waterfalls are seen ahead. Walk above the slate pillars on a faint path to reach a stile in the fence. Go over this and follow the still feint path towards the waterfalls. The path becomes clearer to reach the top of the falls and after an easy scramble the dam holding back the waters of Llyn Cwm Y Foel is reached.

3 Walk across this and BEAR RIGHT at the far side for 30 yards. There are now no paths! Go diagonally up and left towards a shallow grassy gully and walk up the right hand side of it, bearing slightly right to reach

Introduction

The walks in this guide visit some of Snowdonia's most dramatic slate mining areas. These are situated in wonderful mountain and valley scenery and delve into their histories. In their heyday strong communities grew and were mainly Welsh speaking. All these walks reveal the dramatic landscape the quarries and mines were set. Because it took around 10 tons of waste to produce just one ton of usable slate. Huge spoil heaps developed that completely altered the landscape, not only around the villages but in the mountains too. One has only to look at the enormous piles of slate around Blaenau Ffestiniog to appreciate that everything seen on the surface has been brought out from deep down in a mine, all by human endeavour and extremely hard graft. The quarries associated with Llanberis were at one time one of the largest in the world and dramatically scarred the slopes of Elidir Fawr.

It is known that slate has been used since at least Roman times. It is also known that when Richard II arrived in Conwy and its castle was built in 1399 he commented on the fact that many of the houses had much slate on them. Presumably he meant the roofs. However, the main quarrying and mining took place from the end of the 18th century right up until the early 20th century with a few isolated quarries operating to the end of the 1960s. The communities of Gwynedd – Ogwen, Peris, Nantlle, Blaenau Ffestiniog and Corris were dynamic and thriving having between them some 60 quarries and mines that employed over 18,000 people. Paths that were created between villages, hamlets and small towns linked together chapels, schools and the quarries themselves. A word of apology here, the huge Penrhyn Quarry in Bethesda has very little in the way of walks to appreciate this. However, a short one has been included as it was, perhaps the largest quarry in North Wales.

Many of these paths are still in use today whilst some have disappeared altogether. Although much of the infrastructure has disappeared there are the remains of many buildings that once were bustling and noisy. The miners often lived at the mine during the week only returning home on the Saturday afternoon after working their shift. They came back to work very early on Monday morning. Slate is still quarried today but only in small quantities, mainly in the Blaenau Ffestiniog area. When space allows more information is given for each of the walks.

A word of warning here, it is extremely dangerous to enter any of the mines or quarries mentioned in this guide and is NOT recommended unless with a qualified and experienced guide. Spoil heaps are dangerous places too. Slate on these heaps becomes extremely slippery when wet and the many sharp edges can give very nasty cuts.

A number of walks venture into the mountains but only one actually reaches a summit – Walk 3. Mountain weather is very unpredictable. Bad weather springs up unexpectedly and it is wise to be prepared for that. In winter snowfall can be expected, whilst during summer the sun will quickly dehydrate you. Please be aware of these conditions and dress accordingly, as well as taking spare clothing in winter. One item of kit well worth carrying is a group shelter. Coming in different sizes they have proven to be life savers when the weather changes or there is an emergency. Know how to use a map and compass – although a GPS can be used as well you become reliant on a battery for it to work. Mobile phone coverage is often non-existent and cannot be relied upon in the event of an emergency.

Whilst the walks can be followed using the descriptions, provided along with the map, it is always wise to take a map, just in case the mist comes down, and know how to navigate using it. The best ones are the Ordnance Survey Outdoor Leisure, 1:25,000 series. The maps needed for this guide are OL 17 Snowdon/Yr Wyddfa, OL 18 Harlech, Porthmadog & Bala/Y Bala and OL 23 Cadair Idris & Llyn Tegid.

All the walks follow rights of way on paths, tracks or roads. Occasionally paths disappear for short distances but soon re-appear. Many of the walks are away from the more popular areas so meeting people is rare. This gives the walks an air of remoteness and solitude.

You will be awed at the amount of struggle that went in to produce usable material. Think about the sweat and toil involved in extracting the slate and how people lived all those years ago. A trip on any one of the small railways is highly recommended, especially the amazing Ffestiniog, and Welsh Highland, Railways. A visit to one of the show mines is an excellent way to learn about the lives of the quarry workers and their families all those years ago. In the appendix there is a list of other slate based attractions to visit. All that remains is for you to enjoy these walks and have fun.

On a final note there are proposals that the seven main slate areas of North Wales become a UNESCO World Heritage area. These are:

1 Ogwen Valley
2 Dinorwig
3 Nantlle
4 Cwmystradllyn and Cwm Pennant
5 Blaenau Ffestiniog, the Dwyryd and the Ffestiniog Railway
6 Bryn Eglwys, Abergynolwyn and the Talyllyn Railway
7 Aberllefenni

Under the leadership of Gwynedd County Council the nomination has been put together with key partners. The proposal has taken into consideration the variety of technology, organisation, social and environmental impacts of the slate industry in the mountain landscapes on north Wales which once dominated world production.

The key aims of the nomination are:

1 Heritage led regeneration
2 Conservation
3 Economic development

4 Community and skills development
5 Re-connecting communities with heritage
6 Promote and celebrate the important global role of the Welsh slate industry
7 Unified story

It is hoped that UNESCO recognition and inscription will take place in July 2020.

Some interesting facts here about slate include the fact that North Wales' slate is the best in the world. Apart from being very durable it is strong, light and, of course, waterproof.

The output of roofing slate from Gwynedd slate quarries was enough to roof 14 million terraced houses.

The longest industrial dispute in British industrial history was at Penrhyn Quarry just outside Bethesda which lasted for three years starting on the 22nd November 1900. Unfortunately it heralded the demise of the reliability of slate production and orders fell sharply with thousands of workers laid off.

WHAT IS SLATE? ITS FORMATION AND USES

Slate is a metamorphic rock, meaning it has been altered from its original composition. The formation of slate in Snowdonia began around 500 million years ago in the Cambrian period for the Dinorwig, Penrhyn and Nantlle slate and 400 million years ago or Ordovician period for Abergynolwyn, Aberllefenni, Corris and Ffestiniog slate. Originally depositions of fine sediments of clay minerals flaky in character formed a mudstone. Minerals in this determined the colour the slate was eventually going to become. Depositions continued over several million years and huge pressures turned the mudstone into shale.
   Continued pressure and great heat caused a chemical change to occur. The original clay minerals broke down to become other minerals such as mica and feldspar the main constituents of this reformed and different rock, slate. Interestingly the minerals had reformed at an angle to the bedding planes. This was the line of cleavage. Some mines, notably in Gaewern, a part of the Braich Goch mine complex above Corris, have pure white calcite formations such as curtains, stalactites and stalagmites normally only seen in caves.
    The slate above Bethesda and Nantlle tends to have a purple tinge to it, whilst around Blaenau Ffestiniog and Corris it is blue grey and is much finer grained. Generally it is slate from the Cambrian period that provides the most durable and hardest slate. The Blaenau Ffestiniog vein was called the Old Vein and provided excellent slate whist the Corris was named the Narrow Vein and provided excellent slab. Another slate, found outside of Snowdonia (and the coverage of this guide),

was formed in the Silurian period. This is the least durable of the types but it provided good slab for indoor use.

Nowadays slate is used for a plethora of tourist souvenirs, but there have been many other uses. The best snooker tables have slate beds. Other uses apart from roofing slate were: building material, walling, slate plank fencing, flooring, sills, lintels, quoins. It was used to form vats in both the chemical and brewing industries on account of its impervious nature. Cisterns, sold as 'flat packs', were manufactured. In farming it was used in pig sties and cowsheds, dairies and larders not to mention the Victorian 'privy' or gents toilets. It was also used for making coffins, some of which were re-usable (probably for pauper burials) and gravestones. Slate was also used in the electricity trade where it was used for switchboards and insulation.

I have included a list of traditional slate sizes for amusement and it can be seen that their names are predominantly 'female'. *Sizes are in inches.*

Empress 26 x 16

Princess 24 x 14

Duchess 24 x 12

Small Duchess 22 x 12

Marchioness 22 x 11

Broad Countess 20 x 12

Countess 20 x 10

Small Countess 18 x 10

Viscountess 18 x 9

Wide Lady 16 x 10

Broad Lady 16 x 9

Lady 16 x 8

Small Lady 14 x 8

Narrow Lady 14 x 7

Double 12 x 6

Single 10 x 5

Many other sizes and names existed, with over 30 being known at the end of the 19th century. 'Queens' could have been anything from 30 x 18 to 36 x 26 or even larger. 'Princesses' were often termed 'Fourteens'. 'Putts' were 14 x 12 sometimes called 'Headers' and 'Ladies Putts' were 13 x 10, 'Damp Course' slates came in many sizes from 20 x 9 down to 9 x 4½.

WALK I

a path going right to left. Cross this and walk up another shallow gully on a faint path to the lower of the Llynnau Diffwys. A better path continues just below the lake to join another path going right to left. Cross straight over. Fifty yards further on join a very good path. TURN RIGHT and follow it down, but it is often very boggy, to reach a cairn by the side of a good track. TURN LEFT along this heading towards the ruins of Rhosydd Slate Mine. Climb over a ladder stile to view the desolation of a once thriving industry.

4 BEAR RIGHT before entering the ruins and RIGHT again by the gable end of the ruined house. This is to the right of a deeply incised gully above which is a huge spoil heap. A faint path appears then disappears in swampy ground as a ladder stile is approached. Climb over this and BEAR RIGHT on a faint path to avoid the bog and then go left to join the obvious path ahead. Follow this to the partially drained Llyn Croesor. Go through the top of the dam on the walled path. A more gradual ascent now continues to where it descends to the desolate Croesor Slate Mine.

5 Walk through the ruins and climb over a ladder stile on the left. Follow the good track down noting the barred entrance into the mine, DO NOT ENTER, and through a gate above the first farm. The track continues down through another gate to reach a four way junction. Go diagonally right past the houses on the right to a sharp left hand bend. Pass through the gate of the outward walk and continue back to the car park.

Croesor Mine is unusual in that it had little in the way of above ground workings. Worked from the 1850s it closed in 1878 and re-opened in 1895. It produced some 6,000 tons annually but production fell dramatically in the early part of the 20th century. A full scale hydro station was built in 1903 to power the machinery that included ventilation. Work ceased in 1930.

Notes about Rhosydd can be found at the end of the walk description for Walk 3 – Rhosydd.

WALK 2
WRYSGAN MINE

DESCRIPTION This 2 mile walk is full of interest especially on the descent through the surface features of this mine. There are some great views. The walk also visits a very pretty lake, Llyn Wrysgan that supplied water to the mine. Allow at least 1¾ hours for the walk as this gives plenty of time to look around.
DO NOT ENTER ANY OF THE MANY MINE ENTRANCES SEEN ON THIS WALK. They contain much loose debris, have unstable roofs and there are some long drops!
START At the car park where the tarmac ends at the start of the track leading up into Cwmorthin.
DIRECTIONS From the roundabout at the north end of Blaenau Ffestiniog follow the A496 towards Porthmadog for a mile. Turn right towards Tanygrisiau then immediately left towards the power station and Lakeside Cafe. From the south follow the A496 and turn left at the sign for Tanygrisiau and immediately left towards the power station and Lakeside Café. Continue past the café and go around a sweeping right hand bend and over the railway line. Ignoring a left turn leading up to a locked gate, continue straight ahead to a 'T' junction. Turn left and go up to the parking area on the left before some gates. From Porthmadog follow the A487 across The Cob and drive through Penrhyndeudraeth. Continue and pass the Oakley Arms and the turning right to Maentwrog and Harlech. Just beyond this turn left onto the A496 signed for Blaenau Ffestiniog. Keep on this road keeping left at a 'Y' junction to a sign indicating a left turn to Tanygrisiau. Turn left and almost immediately turn left again. Continue as above to the car park.

1 Pass through the kissing gate on the left of the track and follow a path across a footbridge. Note the pretty waterfall. Follow the path to join the access road that goes up to Cwm Stwlan. TURN RIGHT up this and continue past the fine incline that disappears into a tunnel high up the hillside but with a patch of light showing. The road has bisected the incline and the continuation of the incline can be seen plunging down to the left. Continue past a small dam down to the right to where a barred mine entrance is seen 20 yards over to the right. This is some 300yards past the turning on to the road.

2 A faint path bears diagonally left and up away from the road. Follow this until level with the toe of the crag over to the right and where a triangular pinnacle of rock is seen up and left of the crag silhouetted against the sky. BEAR RIGHT and up towards this. At first the path is very faint but becomes clearer to where it arrives at the boulder. This turns out to be just another boulder! Go up slightly leftwards to the obvious wall. This is actually a dam wall holding back the water of Llyn Wrysgan. TURN RIGHT below it. *There is a great view from here of Moelwyn Bach 2,329 feet, the northern end of the Rhinogs and Llyn Trawsfynydd. Over to the east are the Arenigs.* Go up slightly and cross the dam.

3 At the far side go up slightly to a good track and TURN RIGHT below a small spoil heap. Descend this past another small dam to some ruins and a mine entrance on the left. Follow the obvious track to the remains of an old winding house at the top of an incline. *There is a grand view of the spoil heaps of Cwmorthin mine ahead on the far side of the valley.* Descend the incline past another mine entrance on the left to old dressing sheds. TURN LEFT above these. *To the right of the ruined sheds it is possible reach the top end of the tunnel seen earlier in the walk. Here are the remains of the drum gear as well as parts of the steam haulage engine and the remains of a lorry chassis.* At the far side of the ruins bear right through the end ruin. There is another mine entrance over to the left. At the ruined wheel house pass between its walls and descend a staircase to the lowest and flattest area. *This is Cei Mulod, the old landing platform where the donkeys used to gather.*

4 Bear slightly right and descend the obvious path, the old packhorse path, to a track at the bottom. TURN LEFT up this then

WALK 2

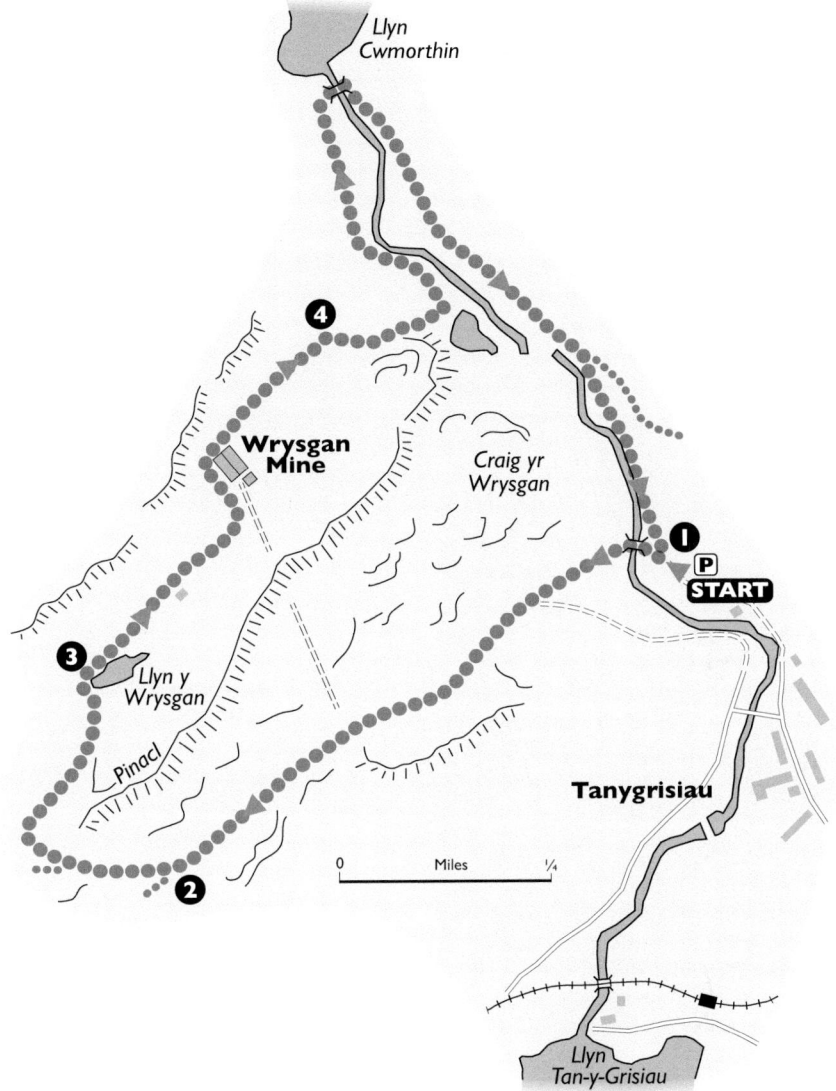

follow it along to a clapper bridge on the right spanning the outflowing stream from Llyn Cwmorthin very close to its end. The ruins of Cwmorthin Terrace are up to the left. Cross the bridge and TURN RIGHT. Follow the track down paralleling the stream back to go through a kissing gate immediately before reaching the car park.

Wrysgan Mine *was first worked in the 1830s with mills opening in 1854 and 1865. The spectacular incline, passed early on in the walk, was built in 1872 and descends some 600 feet to the Ffestiniog Railway. The mine closed in the 1950s. At its peak it produced 3,000 tons of slate in 1904, with around 100 men working on 8 different levels.*

WALK 3
CWMORTHIN, RHOSYDD & WRYSGAN QUARRIES

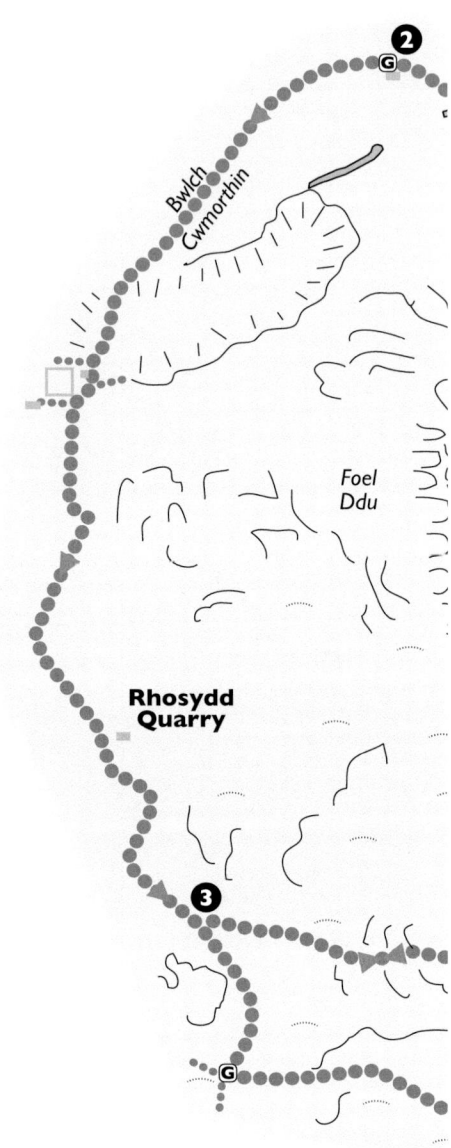

DESCRIPTION This is a superb not to miss 4¾ mile walk visiting 3 quarries with substantial remains. Allow 3½ hours to include some exploration. The panoramic view from the summit of Moel yr Hydd 2,126 feet is superb. Not only does Blaenau Ffestiniog appear to be directly below, from here many of the mountains of Snowdonia are visible. The walk is easily followed on tracks and paths although the section passing below the cliffs of Moel yr Hydd paths are less clear until Llyn Wrysgan is reached. DO NOT ENTER ANY OF THE MANY MINE ENTRANCES SEEN ON THIS WALK. They contain much loose debris, have unstable roofs and there are some long drops!

START At the car park where the tarmac ends at the start of the track leading up into Cwmorthin.

DIRECTIONS Coming from the north on the A470 turn right at the roundabout at the north end of Blaenau Ffestiniog onto the A496 towards Porthmadog. Continue for a mile then turn right towards Tanygrisiau then immediately left through a slate gateway towards the power station and Lakeside Cafe. (From the south turn right, or from Porthmadog left, in Maentwrog onto the A496. Continue towards Blaenau Ffestiniog to the sign for Tanygrisiau. Turn left then immediately left towards the power station and Lakeside Café). Continue past the café and go around a sweeping right hand bend and over the railway line. Continue straight ahead to a 'T' junction. Turn left and go up to the rough parking area on the left before some gates.

Pass through the kissing gate to the right of the wide gate and walk up the track with the tumbling stream on the left and the spoil heap of Cwmorthin Quarry rising chaotically up to the right. Continue straight ahead when the track levels and ignore the track going up to the right to reach a clapper bridge crossing the outflowing stream from Llyn Cwmorthinn. TURN LEFT to cross this then BEAR RIGHT. Pass below the ruins of Cwmorthin Terrace. *These houses were erected by the owners of Cwmorthin Quarry in two stages. The first eight houses were*

WALK 3

■ Plas-cwmorthin

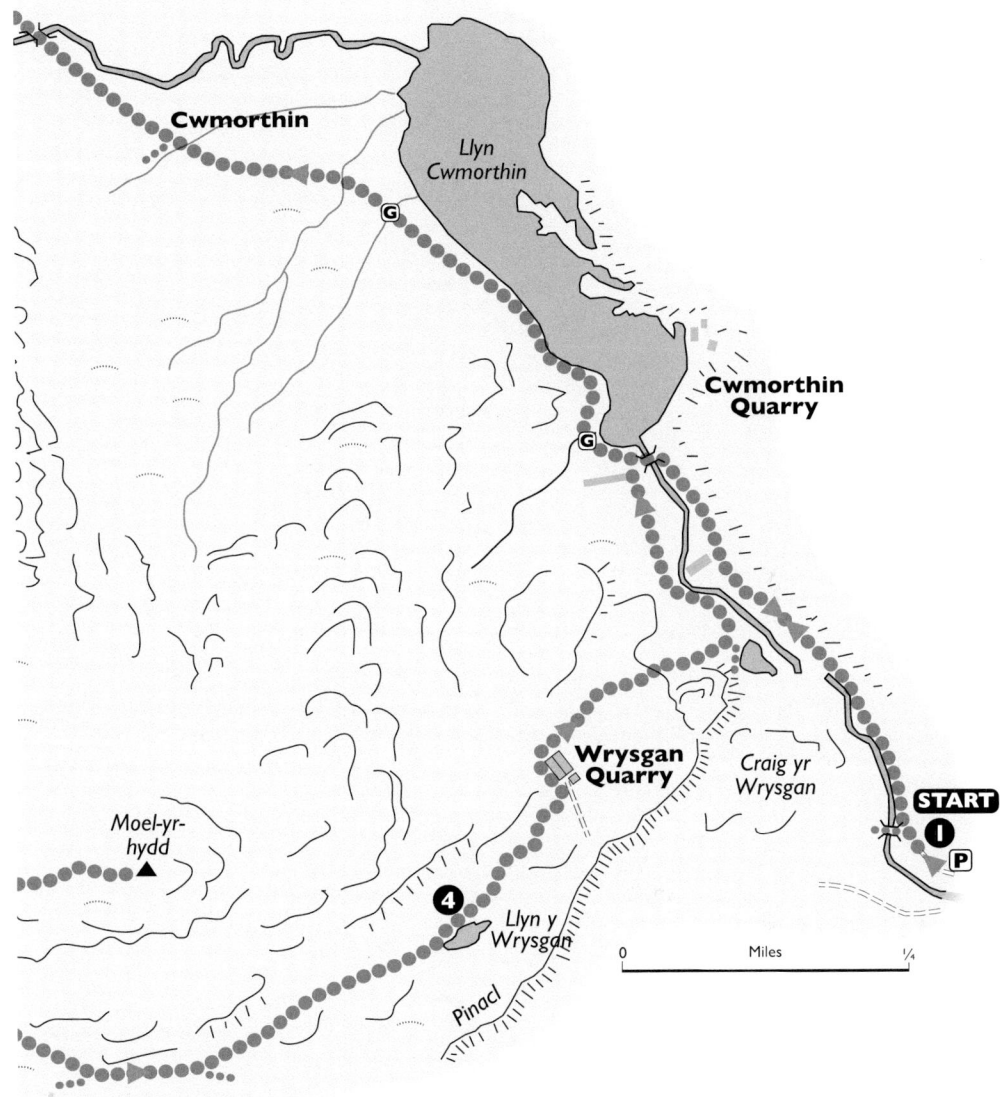

built in the 1860s and a further five in the 1870s. There was nobody living here by the 1930s. Continue through a kissing gate and along the left side of Llyn Cwmorthin to pass through another kissing gate almost opposite the end of the lake. Carry on, not-

ing the fine slate and wire fence to the right, past the ruins of Capel y Gorlan. *This was a Calvinistic Methodist Chapel and built in 1867. There was enough room for 100 worshippers but it closed in the 1930s.* Keep going to where the track ends. *Over to the* right is the ruin of Plas Cwmorthin, once the quarry manager's house. To the left of the track are the ruins of Rhosydd Stables. These were built to shelter the ponies that carried the slate through the valley. It was later extended to provide barracks. Just beyond and where the path starts to rise again over to the left is Rhosydd Terrace. They were built in 1865. In 1881 there were 41 people living here. Interestingly there were 13 people living in number 1!

2 Continue up the steadily rising path after passing through a kissing gate. Close to the top note the wheel pit over to the right. At the top is Rhosydd Quarry where an area of total ruination is seen. Pass through the ruins and follow the obvious incline up that starts to the right of an obvious mine entrance. A stream usually exits here. At the top is the ruin of an old drum house. Bear left and up the next incline with another drum house at the top. *There are great views of Moelwyn Mawr 2,526 feet, from here whilst over to the right is Cnicht 2,260 feet, and Moel Hebog 2,569 feet.* BEAR LEFT and pass to the left of a big boulder and head towards more spoil heaps and ruins. Pass between the heaps noting the remains of roofing slate trimmings. At the ruins BEAR LEFT and up to a large flat area. Bear slightly right and pass in front of a small ruin. Head towards the large pits seen ahead. At a cairn 100 yards before the next ruin a path strikes off to the left.

3 TURN LEFT up this and follow it to reach a fence. Continue up to the summit of Moel yr Hydd. It is a little boggy at the start. *There is a wonderful panoramic view from the unmarked summit. The view clockwise from Moelwyn Bach 2,329 feet, Craigysgafn 2,260 feet, Moelwyn Mawr, Craig Cwm Silyn 2,408 feet, Cnicht, Yr Aran 2,451 feet, Snowdon 3,560 feet, the ridge of Crib Goch, Tryfan 3,010 feet, Glyder Fawr 3,278 feet, Glyder Fach 3,261 feet, the pointed form of Moel Siabod 2,861 feet and Allt Fawr 2,290 feet. To the right of Blaenau Ffestiniog is the rounded lump of Manod Mawr 2,169 feet, Arening Fawr 2,802 feet and the Aran range on the far skyline. To the right of Llyn Trawsfynydd on the skyline is Cadair Idris* 2,930 feet and finally the Rhinogydd. Yr Eifl (The Rivals) on the LLyn Peninsula can be seen to the left of Moel Hebog. Return to the path and TURN LEFT along it to reach a gate. Pass through this. GO LEFT and down gradually passing below the cliffs of Moel yr Hydd. Keep as high as possible and follow the quite faint path along avoiding the obvious descent down the obvious path through boggy ground. Continue to a ruin next to a huge boulder. There is an adit to the left. Keeping left of boggy ground as much as possible continue gradually down to the first dam holding back the water of Llyn Wrysgan. Continue to the left of the lake to another dam.

4 Descend this past to some ruins and a mine entrance on the left. Follow the obvious track to the remains of an old winding house at the top of an incline. *There is a grand view of the spoil heaps of Cwmorthin mine ahead on the far side of the valley.* Descend the incline past another mine entrance on the left to old dressing sheds. TURN LEFT above these. *To the right of the ruined sheds it is possible reach the top end of the incline tunnel. The lower end of it was seen at the top of the incline earlier in the walk. Here are the remains of the drum gear as well as parts of the steam haulage engine and the remnants of a lorry chassis.* At the far side of the ruins bear right through the end ruin. *There is another mine entrance over to the left.* At the ruined wheel house pass between its walls and descend a staircase to the lowest and flattest area. *This is Cei Mulod, the old landing platform where the donkeys used to gather.*

5 Bear slightly right and descend the obvious path, the old packhorse path, to a track at the bottom. TURN LEFT up this then follow it along to a clapper bridge on the right spanning the outflowing stream from Llyn Cwmorthin very close to its end. The ruins of Cwmorthin Terrace are up to the left. Cross the bridge and TURN RIGHT. Follow the track down parallelling the stream back to go through a kissing gate immediately before reaching the car park.

WALK 3

Moelwyn Mawr & ruin

Cwmorthin Mine *commenced quarrying in 1810. Originally a surface operation it was not until the construction of the Ffestiniog Railway that underground mining developed. It was noted as a hazardous mine to work in. In 1882 some 10,376 tons were produced by around 500 men. There was a serious collapse in 1884 and it was connected to Oakeley Mine in 1900. All surface working was then abandoned. In 1970 Cwmorthin and Oakeley closed although there was small scale working in the 1980s and 1990s, the mine finally closed in 1997.*

Rhosydd Mine *started off small in 1830. Unfortunately being high up on the mountain transporting the slate was difficult and made doubly so by the attitude of Cwmorthin Quarry who were reluctant to allow them to use the Ffestiniog Railway. At first transport was by packhorse over the Moelwyns and later by cart or sledge via Cwmorthin. In 1864 the Croesor Tramway was opened which made it much easier to transport the slate. It was the longest single pitch tramway in Wales. Going bust in 1873 the quarry was auctioned in 1874 and became Welsh owned. After a short period of prosperity the threat of World War created a slump in the market and the quarry was closed at the onset of the First World War. It was mothballed and re-opened in 1919 having been bought by the Colman family of mustard fame! They ran it until 1930, mothballed again with final closure in 1948.*

In 1883 the quarry was one of the largest workings in Wales outside of Blaenau Ffestiniog. Its peak was in 1885 when 6,484 tons of finished slates were produced by 207 men. In total during the life of Rhosydd some 222,000 tons of slate was produced, creating spoil heaps that are estimated to have 2.5 million tons of waste!

Many of the workers and their families lived at the site which also had its own chapel. The remains are a stark reminder on how difficult life must have been for these people, living and working here in all weathers – summer and winter.

Wrysgan Mine *was first worked in the 1830s with mills opening in 1854 and 1865. The spectacular incline, passed early on in the walk, was built in 1872 and descends some 600 feet to the Ffestiniog Railway. The mine closed in the 1950s. At its peak it produced 3,000 tons of slate in 1904 by around 100 men working on 8 different levels.*

WALK 4
LEFEL DWR-OER & DIPHWYS QUARRY

DESCRIPTION This 3½ mile walk visits the edges of two quarries visiting some lakes associated with these. Llyn Manod is natural whilst the other two were reservoirs for the slate quarries. Up to the right above Llyn Du-bach are large spoil heaps from the huge Graig Ddu quarry hidden from sight. Interestingly Llyn Glas is now drained of the water supplying Lefel Dwr-oer and the only sign that it was once a lake is the dam and the reeds beyond. Llyn Dwr-oer is surrounded by the remains of quite extensive quarrying. There are some wonderful views of the Moelwyns on this 2½ hour excursion above Blaenau Ffestiniog.
START At the large car park in Cae Clyd
DIRECTIONS Turn off the A470 in Blaenau Ffestiniog onto Cae Clyd. This is opposite the Wynnes Arms at the south end of the town. Follow the narrow road up for 250 yards to a large car park on the right.

1 TURN RIGHT out of the car park and walk up the narrow road ignoring the left turn. Continue straight ahead to where the tarmac ends. Continue along the track, there is a way marker on a lamp post on the left. TURN LEFT 100 yards ahead through the smaller of two gates before reaching the house ahead and follow the track up. TURN RIGHT on a path when the track bears left indicated by the way marker on a fence corner post. Pass through a gate 50 yards ahead. Cross the stone footbridge and go up some steps and follow the partially 'paved' path to go through an old metal gate. Continue straight ahead keeping the wall to the right and pass through a kissing gate. Cross the field straight ahead on a grassy path and step over a low wall. BEAR LEFT to the field corner and go through another kissing gate.

2 Keep the wall, with a fence on top, to the left and follow it around to go through a very old metal gate. Continue up the field still with the wall to the left and through a low wall. *There is a great view of the Moelwyns from here from left to right these are Moelwyn Bach 2,329 feet, Craigysgafn 2,260 feet, Moelwyn Mawr 2,526 feet and Moel yr Hydd 2,126 feet.* Go up to and through a gate in the corner of the field. The wall with the fence on top turns left so continue straight ahead on a boggy path keeping the fence to the left to reach Llyn Manod.

3 TURN RIGHT and follow a faint path some 15 yards away from the lake edge to the far side. TURN LEFT and follow the boggy path keeping above the obvious swampy area to reach the far end of the lake with the start of a fence to the left. A much clearer path continues keeping to the right of the fence. Easy walking continues to where the path starts to descend. Llyn Dwr-oer is seen down to the left and with the Moelwyns forming the skyline. BEAR RIGHT off the path and head towards the obvious incline. Cross this noting the huge fallen slabs of slate, and contour around to the dam that once held back the water in Llyn Glas. BEAR LEFT and keeping high contour around the shallow valley to join a good but narrow grassy path.

4 TURN RIGHT up this and ascend gradually to a way marked gap in the wall on the left. Pass through this. *Note the huge spoil heaps of the Graig-ddu high up to the right.* The larger of the two lakes forming Llyn Du-bach is over to the right. Continue on a path bearing slightly leftwards at first then rightwards to the smaller lake. TURN LEFT on an indistinct path 100 yards before the obvious kissing gate. Follow this path to reach a fence and a way marked stile. Climb over this and follow the still indistinct path and CAREFULLY cross the stream. The path becomes gradually clearer and continues below spoil heaps. After a short ascent the path joins another. Continue

WALK 4

ahead and down passing to the right of a rocky bluff. Follow the very old tramway down towards the small conifer plantation seen ahead. BEAR RIGHT 200 yards before this to the fence on the right and continue down past a way mark to reach a track. TURN RIGHT and follow it down to a kissing gate.

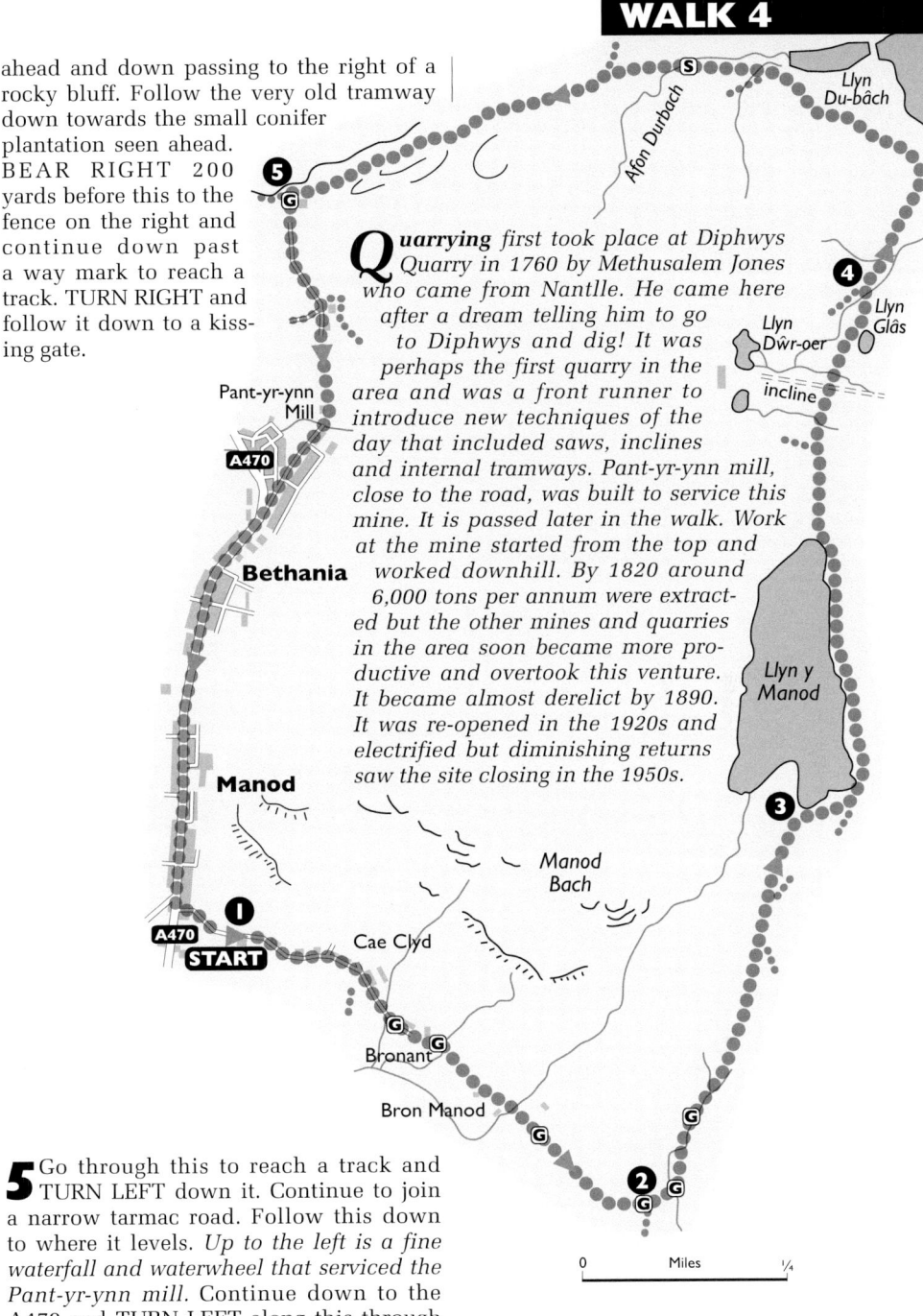

Quarrying first took place at Diphwys Quarry in 1760 by Methusalem Jones who came from Nantlle. He came here after a dream telling him to go to Diphwys and dig! It was perhaps the first quarry in the area and was a front runner to introduce new techniques of the day that included saws, inclines and internal tramways. Pant-yr-ynn mill, close to the road, was built to service this mine. It is passed later in the walk. Work at the mine started from the top and worked downhill. By 1820 around 6,000 tons per annum were extracted but the other mines and quarries in the area soon became more productive and overtook this venture. It became almost derelict by 1890. It was re-opened in the 1920s and electrified but diminishing returns saw the site closing in the 1950s.

5 Go through this to reach a track and TURN LEFT down it. Continue to join a narrow tarmac road. Follow this down to where it levels. *Up to the left is a fine waterfall and waterwheel that serviced the Pant-yr-ynn mill.* Continue down to the A470 and TURN LEFT along this through the town to the Wynnes Arms. TURN LEFT up Cae Clyd back to the car park.

WALK 5
MAEN-OFFEREN & DIPHWYS QUARRIES

DESCRIPTION This is a very interesting 4 mile walk that also has some tremendous views. It passes through the quarries and the upper part of Llechwedd Slate Mines. Away from the quarries there is a sense of remoteness. There is a short pathless section but that is easily passed. Allow 2¾ hours.

START At the main car park, close to the 'Antur Stiniog' café and shop in the centre of Blaenau Ffestiniog.

DIRECTIONS From the north or the south follow the A470 into Blaenau Ffestiniog. Opposite the turning down to the station turn left, if coming from the north, or right if coming from the south to park in the large car park close to 'Antur Stniog' where a small fee is payable. There are toilets.

1 Walk out of the car park past the toilets. Keeping to the right of the car park, go up to the top right hand side and up a short rise to a road, Lord Street. Turn left along this then go steeply up to where the tarmac ends at a gate and a kissing gate to the left of it. Pass through this and follow the track up to a marker post on the left to where the track levels. Continue straight ahead following the marker posts through the working area to where a grassy track continues ahead. DO NOT follow the quarry road from this point.

2 Follow the grassy track passing banks of gravel to a finger post. Bear left and walk gradually up between rhododendron bushes to a marker post. The path now zigs to the right then zags to the left and continues through more rhododendron bushes to another marker post. Go up to the right quite steeply to the next marker post to where it levels and goes right. Go along to the next marker post up to the left 60 yards further. Turn left up a quite steep path passing marker posts to where the path more or less levels and contours the hillside past marker posts to arrive at a drum house.

3 Carefully climb up the loose but short slate slope on the right up to a quarry road, CARE. Turn right and some 30 yards further turn left up an obvious but less well used track. When this ends a wide grassy path/track bears right then goes back left towards the obvious pipe. Keeping below this continue to the remains of a once fine, remote drum house on the right. Continue to the obvious gate. Climb over the fine slate stone step stile to the continuation of the path/track.

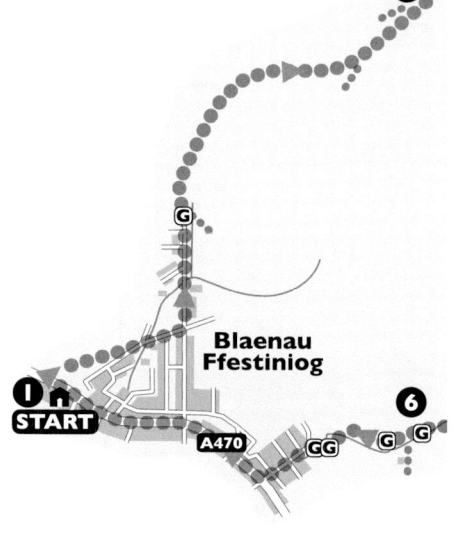

4 Follow this to the dam holding back the water of Llyn Newydd on the left. This is just before two upended concrete pipes. Leave the track and walk up to the lake. Return to the track and turn left. Walk down into a dip and back up again. Continue to where Llyn Bowydd suddenly appears. Walk along the top of the dam until it ends. Turn sharp right and down a vague path. The path becomes lost so continue around a rocky knoll and then bear left to a substantial wall on your left. Follow this by going slightly up and then down to a way marked ladder stile. Climb over this to reach a path. This veers away from the wall and continues to a dilapidated stile just before Llyn Drum-boeth.

WALK 5

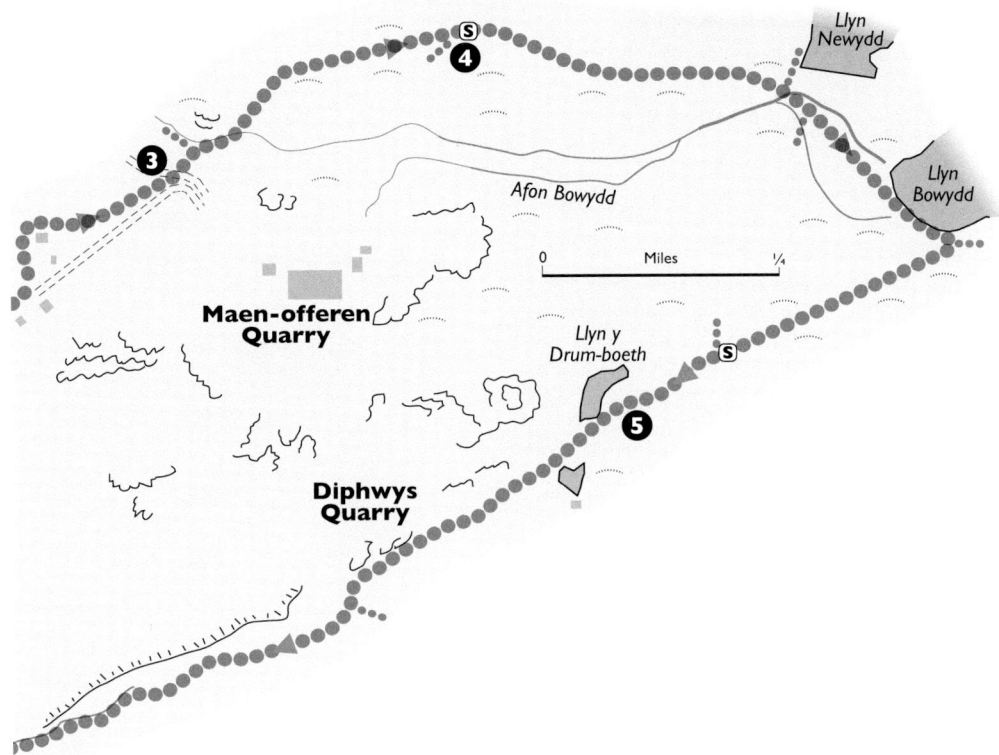

5 It is safer to cross the fallen wall. Bear left on a much more defined path through small spoil heaps alongside Diphwys Quarry with increasingly glorious views. The path continues along the level top of a spoil heap to where a steep descent leads down, CARE as slate is sharp and can cause nasty cuts, and continues to another winding house, way marker. Walk down the incline to a stone hut on the right. Turn left here down some steps. Follow the good path bearing right. Pass to the right of a grassy/rock knoll and walk down a system of inclines heading towards the right edge of a conifer plantation ahead. When you reach the track above it turn right and follow it down to a gate.

6 Go through this. Turn left. Pass through a small ornate one on the right 15 yards further. Follow the path down to a fence and continue down to where the path veers right to a gate to the left of a house. Go though this and another 20 yards further to reach a road. Walk straight ahead down the steep road to the A470. There is a helpful railing on the right. Turn right along this back to the car park.

Maen-offeren started life in the early 1800s. At first it did not produce very much but by the 1850s it became very successful, producing a creditable total of 14,000 tons per annum whilst employing over 400 men. Electricity was introduced in the 1890s with hydro electricity used from 1918 and remaining in use until 1980. It was the last totally underground working quarry in the area. It was also a pioneer in the use of wire saws. The quarry finally closed in 2001. Unfortunately not very much can be seen on the surface.

WALK 6
HAFODLAS QUARRY

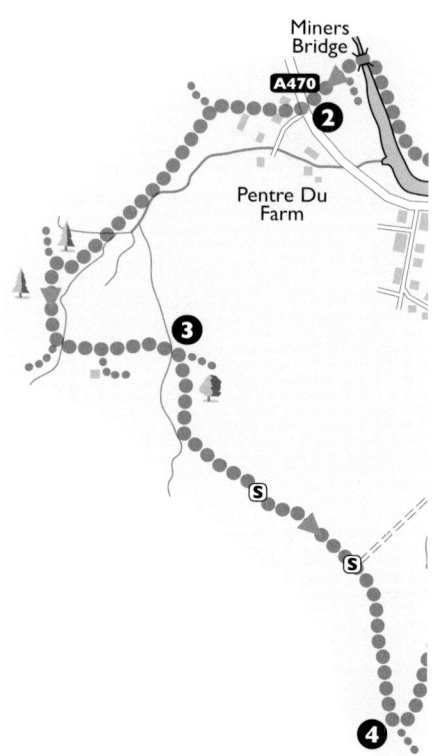

DESCRIPTION This is a very pleasant 2¾ mile walk. It initially follows the Afon Llugwy to where it crosses the Llugwy on the Miners Bridge to reach the A5. The walk continues past a small but pretty waterfall and passes through lovely forestry and woodland. Although there are no stark remains I have included this quarry to show how nature can repair damage to the land once man has gone. The remains of the workings are mostly hidden by trees whilst the pits are completely tree filled. On return the walk passes through more forestry and woodland back to the A5. This is followed a short distance back into Betws-y-Coed. Allow 1¾ hours.

START At the Pont y Pair car park in Betws y Coed

DIRECTIONS Leave the A5 in the village onto the B5106 that leads to Trefriw. Immediately after crossing the bridge over the Afon Llugwy turn left into the car park where a fee is payable but there are toilets.

1 Cross the road from the car park and TURN RIGHT to the information panel and finger post. Follow the gravel path onto a section of duckboards and continue to a 'Y' junction. BEAR LEFT towards the river to a fine picnic area. Follow the riverside path to pass through a kissing gate. Keep following the path alongside the Afon Llugwy across the meadow and pass through another kissing gate. The path becomes rougher as it follows a fence to the left to reach the Miner's Bridge. Ascend this fine feature and continue up to the A5. Cross over – CAEFULLY

2 TURN RIGHT up the steep road to where the tarmac ends at the start of a forest track. TURN LEFT on the path leaving the turning/parking area and walk very gradually up on a good path to cross a footbridge over a stream. Continue up to the small but pretty Garth waterfall. Bear right and ascend much more steeply to arrive at a forest track. There is a 'shark's fin' of rock to the right. TURN LEFT up the track and cross the bridge spanning the stream. Carry on up to a cross roads of tracks. IGNORE the one going up to the right and the one to the left going down. Continue straight ahead on the level track for 200 yards and TURN RIGHT 15 yards beyond a tiny stream.

3 Follow this obvious path through the wood to reach a stile. To the right is a spoil heap. Continue straight ahead to a low boulder and carry on to a large oak on the right. BEAR RIGHT and continue to climb over a stile with a locked gate to the right. Bear right and up to pass by some ruins to cross a dilapidated bridge over a stream. There is an adit to the right. Go steeply up to an old track with a padlocked gate on the right. TURN LEFT then TURN RIGHT 25 yards further with the fence. Follow the fence keeping it to the right. Continue up to

WALK 6

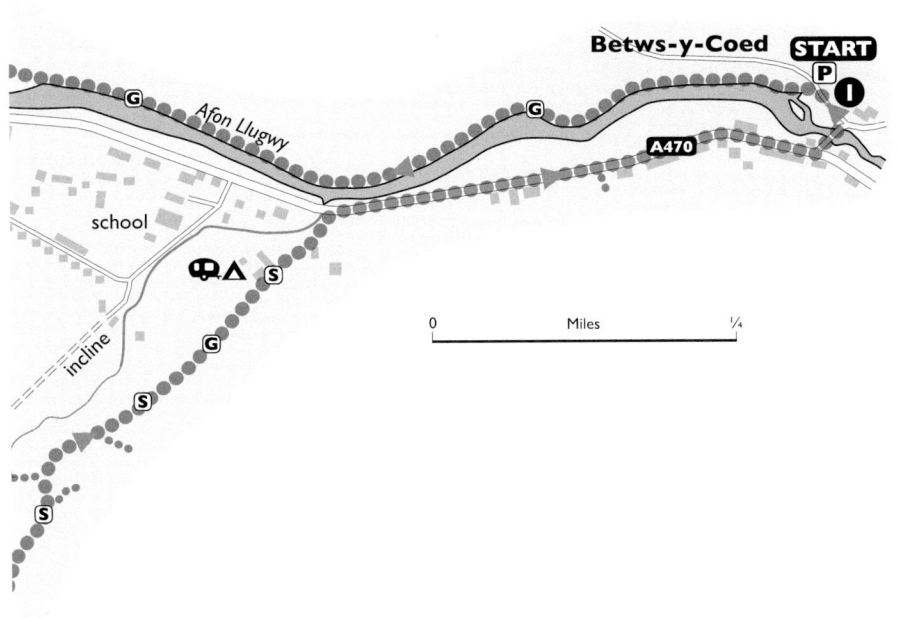

the large pit on the right. *Notice how nature has reclaimed what must have been quite a stark place when quarrying ceased.* Carry on up to the junction with a wide path.

4 TURN LEFT and follow this down to a 'T' junction. IGNORE the left turn. Continue straight ahead downhill and climb over a stile. BEAR LEFT and down track/path for 10 yards and TURN LEFT on a narrow path. Descend this quite steeply to climb over a ladder stile. Continue much more gradually down the pretty walled track. Pass through a gate and then over a stile (or through the gate) to reach a track. TURN RIGHT along this to reach the A5. TURN RIGHT to return to the car park.

*D**eveloped** in the mid 18th century, Hafodlas was expanded at great cost towards the end of that century. In 1883 eleven quarrymen produced 289 tons. However, during that period tonnage was increased to around 2,000 by producing sills for local properties. There were six levels and two pits side by side of each other. Initially the finished product was sent to Trefriw but later to Betws-y-Coed. It was one of the very few quarries to enamel slate on site. After the decline pre-World War I work commenced after hostilities ceased, but it closed in 1929.*

*T**he Douglas Firs** were planted as young saplings in the 1920s. They now weigh over 10 tons each.*

*P**ont y Pair**, the Bridge of the Cauldron, was designed and partially built by Howell the mason from Bala. He died around 1475. It was around this feature that the village grew. In spate the cauldron effect is obvious. Traffic often grinds to a halt here as scores of people stare at the waterfalls and crashing water from the bridge.*

WALK 7
DINORWIG QUARRY

DESCRIPTION This is a superb 4¼ mile walk that traverses one of the largest slate quarries in Wales. It beggars belief that everything seen on the spoil heaps has been put there by human endeavour. The huge pit of Matilda Quarry is truly spectacular and the many inclines are a testimony to the quarrymen's ingenuity. Views of the surrounding mountains are spectacular as well as ones to Llanberis and Llyn Padarn. Part of the Dinorwig Nature Reserve with fine sessile oaks is descended past the Anglesey barracks to follow an amazing walled path down to the road. A visit is made to Dolbadarn Castle before walking back along the A4086 on a good footpath back to the car park. Allow 3 hours.

START At a car park, a loop of the old road, close to the end of Llyn Peris.

DIRECTIONS From Llanberis follow the A4086 towards Nant Peris and Llanberis Pass. As the road descends towards the end of Llyn Peris a large layby will be seen to the right of the road where there is plenty of room for parking. This car park will be on the left when coming from Pen y Pass just beyond Nant Peris.

1 Cross the road from the car park and TURN RIGHT along the footpath towards Nant Peris for 250 yards to an access road with a bridleway finger post. TURN LEFT through the gate and follow the tarmac road to reach a 'Y junction. Go up the left arm of the 'Y' and pass through a kissing gate at the start of a rough track where the tarmac ends. Follow the track up as it steepens by the first spoil heap. Continue up to where it levels briefly. *This is New York Level.* The track swings right and goes up less steeply. *Up to the right forming the skyline is Crib Goch.* When the track switchbacks left there is a fine view of Moel Eilio 2,382 feet. Continue 'a zigging and a zagging' up through this incredible and ruinous landscape to a huge deep pit. Pass between high walls and continue along a level track to where it descends slightly into a dip. *There is a hidden quarry pool, although often just a muddy or dry hollow, to the right beyond the substantial fencing!* Go up to where the track levels and bears left. Note the fine incline going up to the right. Continue to a kissing gate.

2 Pass through this. *Note the ruined large mill over to the right.* TURN LEFT and continue to a very fine view point. *The mountains forming the skyline are, left to right, Crib y Ddysgl 3,494 feet at the end of Crib Goch and close to the summit of Snowdon which it hides. To the right is Moel Cynghorion 2,211 feet, Foel Goch 1,985 feet, Foel Gron 2,064 feet and Moel Eilio.* Return to the kissing gate. TURN RIGHT through the kissing gate immediately in front of the one just passed through. The path bears right and continues down the straight incline with a fence to the left and passes between high slate walls. *Note the frequent holes in the slate that housed the holding brackets for the incline rails as well as lengths of the 'I' section line, the rollers and occasional lengths of wire.* Pass between more walls to where the path levels and reaches a drum house. Bear right and step through a low wall and pass to the right of house. TURN LEFT and keep following the fence down passing several blue ringed marker posts to where it is possible to TURN RIGHT through a wide doorway to view Anglesey Barracks.

3 Return to the path and continue down the incline to where it levels and bears right. Carry on until below an ancient metal footbridge with a ruined drum house just beyond it. Go up to the right immediately before going underneath the bridge.to a clear path. TURN LEFT across the bridge to a remarkable walled path. Follow this down to where it leaves it to descend a steep slope interspersed with irregular slate steps and a final short section of walled path to reach the road. TURN RIGHT to the roundabout then TURN LEFT and follow the footpath until opposite the car park for Dolbadarn Castle.

4 TURN LEFT. Cross the footbridge and go through the kissing gate. Continue up the roughly tarmacked path to climb a short flight of steps to reach wall. Pass through

WALK 7

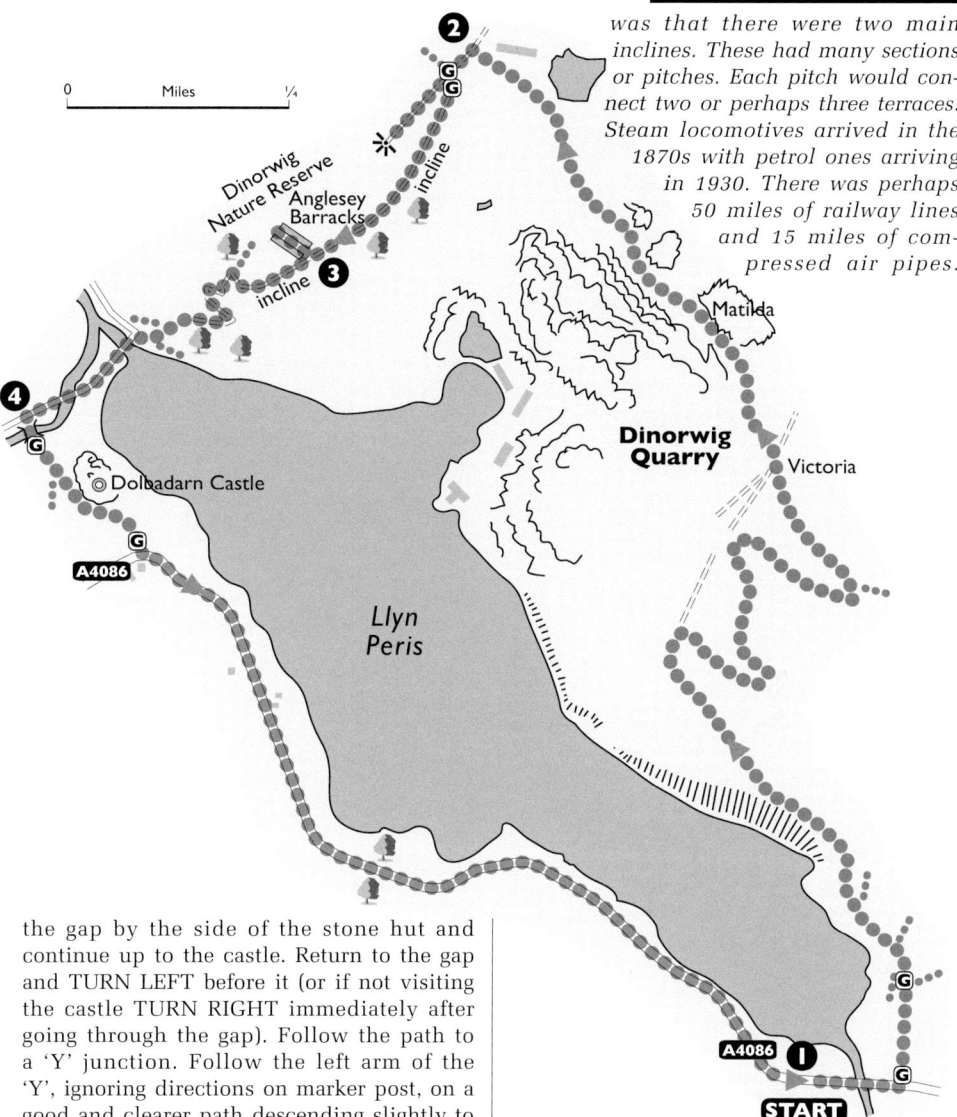

was that there were two main inclines. These had many sections or pitches. Each pitch would connect two or perhaps three terraces. Steam locomotives arrived in the 1870s with petrol ones arriving in 1930. There was perhaps 50 miles of railway lines and 15 miles of compressed air pipes.

the gap by the side of the stone hut and continue up to the castle. Return to the gap and TURN LEFT before it (or if not visiting the castle TURN RIGHT immediately after going through the gap). Follow the path to a 'Y' junction. Follow the left arm of the 'Y', ignoring directions on marker post, on a good and clearer path descending slightly to go through a kissing gate to a track. TURN RIGHT up the track to reach the A4086. TURN LEFT along this back to the car park.

*A*ssheton-Smith the landowner started slate quarrying here in 1782. By the turn of the century there were 13 levels some 60 to 75 feet high. The first incline was built in 1789 but sledges were more often used until 1816. One of the features of Dinorwig Quarry

The main mill was on a level with Dinorwig village and is best seen when walking back from the viewpoint. 'Blondins' were installed in the 1930s and electric power came from Cwm Dyli in 1905. The quarry's output in the late 1890s was 100,000 tons per annum. That produced a million tons of waste to be scattered over the slopes of Elidir Fawr! Almost 3,000 workers were employed at that time. Work stopped in 1969.

WALK 8

VIVIAN & DINORWIG QUARRY HOSPITAL

DESCRIPTION This is a very pleasant and quite easy one mile walk taking in the flooded pit of Vivian Quarry, part of the A1 incline and the Quarry Hospital. There is a great view of the surrounding mountains, Llanberis and Llyn Padarn from the hospital. This is well worth a visit. There is original gruesome medical equipment from the 1800's along with a ward, operating theatre an original X-Ray machine and a mortuary. The photographic exhibition depicts pictures of the quarrymen and memorabilia from local poet and dramatist T Rowland Hughes. Opening times vary, but it is *generally open 7 days a week from the end of May to early September*. Check for other opening times. The walk occupies no more 45 minutes but allow a good 2 hours at least for sightseeing and a visit to the Quarry Hospital.

START At the Gilfach Ddu car park, Llanberis close to the National Slate Museum.

DIRECTIONS From Llanberis follow signs to the National Slate Museum and the car park where a fee is payable but there are toilets and of course the Museum is on hand as well as the terminus of the Llanberis Lake Railway.

Walk out of the car park towards the Llanberis Lake Railway. Cross the line and continue to the dive centre. Pass through the fine arch to the right into Vivian Quarry. Follow the path to a viewing platform where divers below and climbers above may be seen. *Note the Blondin (chain incline) dangling over the water.* Return through the arch and TURN LEFT up the side of the cleaned A1 incline. Where the 'cleaned' section ends TURN LEFT through the gap in the wall to a road. TURN LEFT up this past viewpoint 1 where it is possible to look down into Vivian Quarry. Keep following the road and pass below the V2 incline noting the fine slate wall to the right. Continue up to the hospital. *There are fine views from here of Llanberis and mountains above it. These are right to left Moel Eilio 2,382 feet, Foel Gron 2,064 feet, Foel Goch 1,985 feet and Moel Cynghorion 2,211 feet. Snowdon 3,560 feet is over to the left. Over to the right of Moel Eilio and much lower down the spoil heaps of Glynrhonwy Quarries are easily seen.* After visiting and admiring the fine view, descend the steps in front of the hospital to another lovely viewpoint. Follow the path down to a track and keeping left continue to the railway and the car park noting the fine V2 incline up to the left on the way.

A leaflet can be obtained in the information kiosk in the car park. Below are some interesting facts about the area.

A part of the gigantic Dinorwig Quarry, work in Vivian Quarry ceased in 1958. It shared all the facilities of Dinorwig but was classed as separate from it. The water is around 60 feet deep.

The V2 incline was completed in 1873 and continued in service until the 1920s. The wagons had a level base and slates were loaded on to one of the wagons. The loaded wagon travelled down whilst the empty one went up. The incline was restored in 1998. The width of each track is 5ft 6ins with both having a gradient of 1:1.3.

Blondins are specialised forms of Chain Inclines. They allow loads to be picked up and transported and set down at any point along it.

Slate had many uses and apart from the obvious ones of slates for roofs and as building material it was used for the beds for snooker tables, cosmetics, building roads, walls, fences, homeopathic remedies, gravestones and cisterns. All the best snooker tables have slate beds! Slate from the Llanberis quarries was exported worldwide.

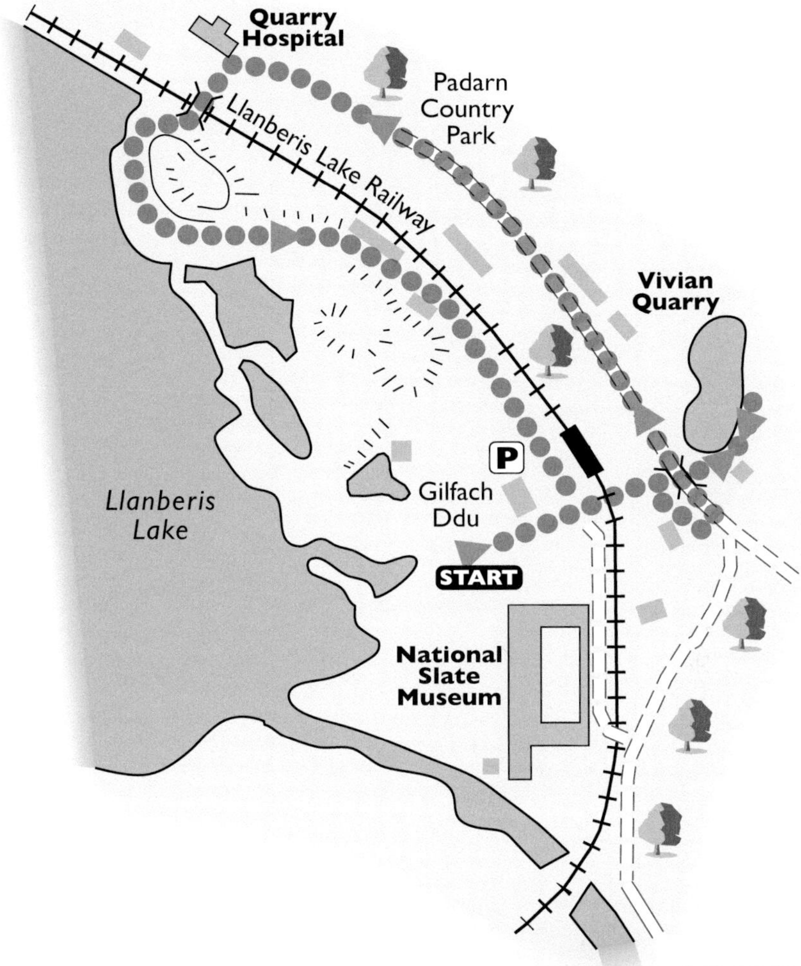

WALK 8

The Quarry Hospital

WALK 9
AROUND VIVIAN QUARRY

DESCRIPTION This is a great 1¾ mile walk taking in the flooded pit of Vivian Quarry part of the A1 incline and several drum houses. The walk from the upper one is through fine sessile oak woodland floored with bluebells in spring. The Anglesey Barracks are a stark reminder of how the quarrymen lived and worked. There is a great view of the surrounding mountains, Llanberis and Llyn Padarn from the top of the incline before going into the woodland. The walk is easily followed on clear paths and tracks. The paths are often steep in ascent and very steep on descent with irregular steps where care is needed especially in wet weather. Allow 2 hours.
START At the Gilfach Ddu car park, Llanberis close to the National Slate Museum.
DIRECTIONS From Llanberis follow signs to the National Slate Museum and the car park where a fee is payable but there are toilets and of course the Museum is on hand as well as the terminus of the Llanberis Lake Railway.

1 Walk out of the car park towards the Llanberis Lake Railway. Cross the line and continue to the dive centre. Pass through the fine arch to the right into Vivian Quarry. Follow the path to a viewing platform where divers below and climbers above may be seen. Note the 'Blondin' dangling over the water. Return through the arch and TURN LEFT up the side of the cleaned A1 incline. Where the 'cleaned' section ends continue up to the drum house seen at the top. There is a fine example of the braking mechanism as well as the drum. Keep following the incline steeply up to another but much more ruinous one. Continue below the drum and footbridge. TURN LEFT immediately beyond the bridge and go up to a marker post. *Going over the footbridge to the start of a fine walled path there are superb views of the mountains, Llanberis and Llyn Padarn. The mountains are from left to right, Moel Cynghorion 2,211 feet, Foel Goch 1,985 feet, Foel Gron 2,064 feet and the massive looking Moel Eilio 2,328 feet.*

2 Having admired the view return over the bridge and continue up the path through very fine sessile oak woodland a part of the Dinorwig Nature Reserve. Bluebells carpet the ground in spring. Continue up to a path that goes off to the right. TURN RIGHT here to view the Anglesey Barracks. Return to the path and continue up steeply to reach a level track going off to the right. IGNORE this. Go up to the left and continue up to go through a gap in a low wall. TURN LEFT and pass an information panel. Follow the level path to where it rises again and passes above the impressive gash of Vivian Quarry. *There are more amazing views of Llanberis and mountains including Snowdon 3,560 feet.* Continue along and up to reach a track.

3 TURN LEFT along it, a part of the old tramway. On a low wall before a higher one is a fine circular etching. TURN LEFT 100 yards further on past the low wall where there is a marker post. Follow the path down keeping the fence to the left to a kissing gate. Pass through this and follow the path to the right and go over a ladder stile. Continue to a 'T' junction. TURN LEFT and down. Marker posts lower down confirm the correct way has been taken! At the 'Y' junction TURN LEFT as indicated by the marker post and continue down through more fine sessile oak woodland. Continue straight ahead at the red topped marker post. At the next path junction go up to the left and then go along to a drum house. Continue above it on a level path to the edge of Vivian Quarry,

4 Descend a series of very steep and irregular slate steps, CARE especially in wet weather. At the base of these bear left at marker posts and descend three more series of very steep slate steps again taking care. At the top of the third set there is a fine view of the quarry. Climbers can often be seen gathered on the ledges, usually in summer, contemplating their next moves! Descend more steps to a reach a level track. TURN LEFT and pass ruins. Continue down past another

WALK 9

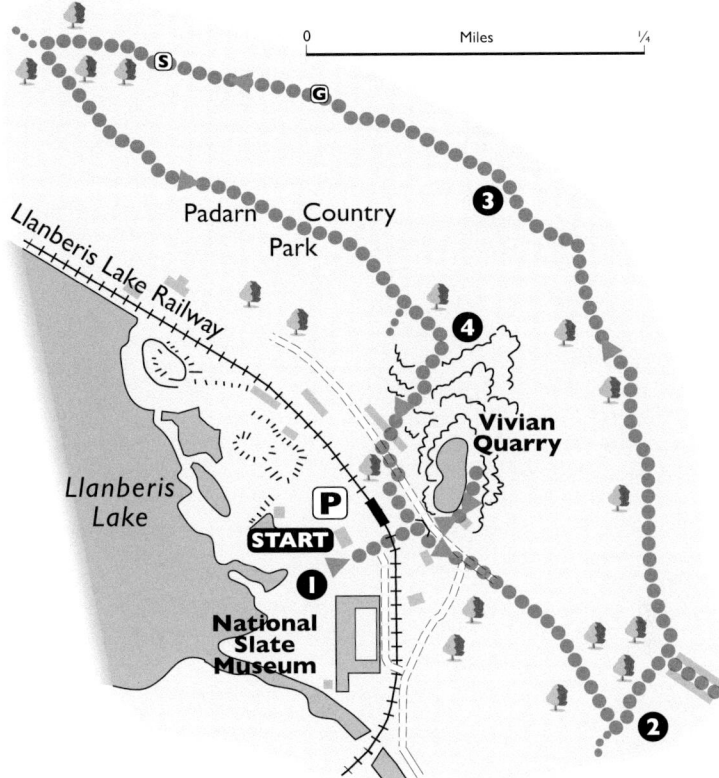

great view of the quarry again and descend an easier angled set of steps to reach a road. This leads up to the hospital. TURN LEFT down the road then TURN RIGHT through a gap in the wall 25 yards further. Descend yet more steps to reach the rear of the Llanberis Lake Railway café and ticket office. TURN LEFT then RIGHT to return to the car park.

A leaflet can be obtained in the information kiosk in the car park. Below are some interesting facts about the area.

A part of the gigantic Dinorwig Quarry, work in Vivian Quarry ceased in 1958. It shared all the facilities of Dinorwig but was classed as separate from it. The water is around 60 feet deep.

The V2 incline was completed in 1873 and continued in service until the 1920s. The wagons had a level base and slates were loaded on to one of the wagons. The loaded wagon travelled down whilst the empty one went up. The incline was restored in 1998. The width of each track is 5ft 6ins with both having a gradient of 1:1.3.

Blondins are specialised forms of Chain Inclines. They allow loads to be picked up and transported and set down at any point along it.

Slate had many uses and apart from the obvious ones of slates for roofs and as building material it was used for the beds for snooker tables, cosmetics, building roads, walls, fences, homeopathic remedies, gravestones and cisterns. All the best snooker tables have slate beds! Slate from the Llanberis quarries was exported worldwide.

WALK 10

PENRHYN QUARRY, BETHESDA

DESCRIPTION This is a pleasant 3¾ mile walk for which 2 hours should suffice. Although it does not visit the workings the spoil heaps and associated ruins are extensive. Part of the walk is on the Lon Las Ogwen cycle route. There is lovely woodland and the tumbling Afon Ogwen is present for much of the walk. There is a short section from leaving Lon Las Ogwen through fields and woodland that is followed on a faint path otherwise there is track and road walking. A visit to Zip World allows the huge quarry to be appreciated after the walk. Although half the walk is outside the National Park I have included it as it is a great part of the Snowdonia's slate heritage and part of the walk is also a part of 'The Slate Trail', a circular walk of 85 miles through the National Park visiting the major slate mining areas.

START Roadside parking close to the bridge over the Afon Ogwen.

DIRECTIONS Turn off the A5 onto the B4409 at signs for Zip World. This turning is on the left before entering Bethesda when coming from the Betws y Coed direction or on the right leaving Bethesda when going towards Betws y Coed. There is room for several cars before crossing the road bridge on the left or right 100 yards after leaving the A5.

1 Walk across the bridge and TURN LEFT up the access road towards Zip World. TURN LEFT through the gate on the left after 350 yards. This is part of Lon Las Ogwen, a part of the National Cycle Network, route 82. There is also an information panel on the right and a roundel for the 'Slate Trail'. Follow the wide gravel track up to a slight rise and where there are some pretty cataracts to the left in the Afon Ogwen. There is also a seat here. Continue up and along the track with spoil heaps to right to Pont Ogwen. DO NOT cross the bridge but go through the gate straight ahead and continue up the rising path/track to go through another gate. Continue along the track with tall spoil heaps to the right. *There is a good view of Pen yr Ole Wen 3,209 feet ahead.* The undulating path/track continues, sometimes gravel, sometimes tarmacked with huge spoil heaps with ruins on top of them to the right. *Further along Glyder Fach 3,261 feet, Glyder Fawr 3,278 feet, Carnedd y Filiast 2,694 feet and Mynydd Perfedd 2,664 feet come into view to the right.* Keep following the path/track to go through a gate from where Tryfan 3,010 feet is visible to reach a narrow road.

2 TURN LEFT down this and follow it to a 90 degrees right hand bend. Pass through the gate on the left and follow the access track until it starts to descend to a small group of cottages. TURN RIGHT onto a faint path and follow it down to the wall. TURN LEFT alongside it and follow the still faint path across a small 'clapper bridge'. Keeping close to the wall on the right continue to climb over a ladder stile. Bear slightly right and go up close to the wall and continue to reach a much clearer path. TURN RIGHT and carry on to a 'Y' junction. Go down the right arm of the 'Y' towards the farm to an old metal gate on the right. Pass through this and TURN LEFT to pass above the farm to reach the access track. Follow this through a gate to the bridge over the Afon Ogwen. Go through the gate and cross the bridge and continue to the A5.

3 TURN LEFT along the footpath by the side of the road and continue to the access road for Ogwen Bank. TURN LEFT down this and cross Pont Ogwen to reach the gravel track of the outward walk. TURN RIGHT and retrace steps back to the car parking area.

*Q**uarrying started here around the 1500s but the present workings date back to 1782. It grew quickly and in 10 years tonnages were in five figures whilst in the latter part of the 19th century annual tonnages were over 100,000. The peak was in 1882 when the 2089 men produced 111,666 tons – just that year alone produced well over a million tons of waste material! I wonder how*

WALK 10

million tons of waste there are in total? The gallery method of mining was introduced in 1789 to facilitate more men working. These were set out at around 65 – 70 feet intervals. In all there were 21 of these galleries each having its own rail system. Before slate was shipped from the port at Penrhyn, constructed in 1790 along with a writing slate factory, the slate went to Bangor for shipment. In 1801 the horse and gravity Penrhyn Railroad replaced 140 men, along with 400 wagons, who, until then had been involved with carting the slate. The Railroad was replaced in 1878 by the Penrhyn Railway. The quarry is still worked in part today and the exhilarating Velocity zip line operated by Zip World can be found here.

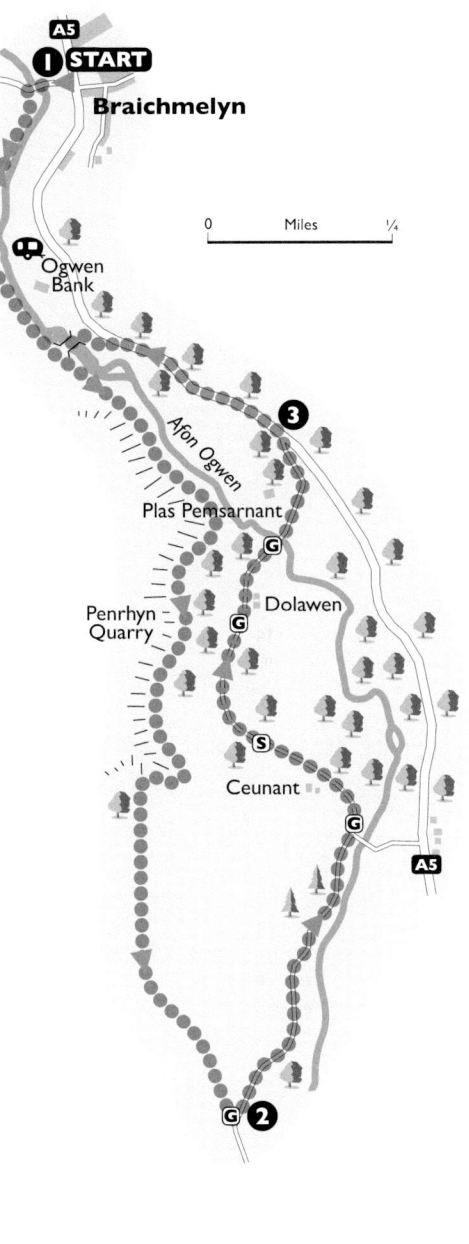

The Slate Man at Zip World

25

WALK 11
GOLWERN QUARRY

DESCRIPTION Initially following Ffordd Panteinion past the verdant Henddol waterfall this fine 3 mile walk follows green paths, part of a higher ancient mountain road system, to gain height. The walk then goes across the hillside through woodland to descend through the long disused Golwern quarry workings. The return walk passes through some fine stone built features down a steep access track. Access to the Blue Lake is no longer possible. Allow 2½ hours.
START At the large layby close to the Sea View guest house.
DIRECTIONS From Dolgellau follow the A493 towards Tywyn. Drive past the turning to Fairbourne to where Ffordd Panteinion is noticed on the left ¼ mile further. There is a phone box opposite this. The layby is another 100 yards further on the right or if that is full there is parking on the left a little further. Coming from Tywyn on the A493 drive into Friog to where the Sea View guest house is seen to the left. Either park on the right before it or continue to the layby on the left 50 yards further on.

1 Walk towards Fairbourne and TURN RIGHT up Ffordd Panteinion. There is also a finger post for the Wales Coastal Path. Cross over and walk up this dead end road to a sharp left hand bend. On the right here is a very pretty waterfall. A better view can be obtained by stepping down to the stream and crossing over. *The short scramble up on the far side is slippery so care needs to be taken.* Return to the road and continue up it to just before Panteinion Hall. TURN VERY SHARPLY RIGHT on the signed path through the gate. Follow the track up to pass through a kissing gate. The path rises steadily with a fence to the left to reach a 'Y' junction. Go up the right arm of the 'Y' and climb quite steeply up to go through a gate. *There are glimpses through the trees of the southern arm of the Rhinogydd up this path.* The path bears right and goes up to a small spoil heap.

BEAR RIGHT below this and then go up to the right of it to some ruins from which there is a great view of Fairbourne and the Llyn Peninsula. The path continues up and as height is gained Barmouth comes into view down to the left, a fine vista. Pass through a gap then continue up the walled path or across the top edge of the field keeping a wall to the left to a marker post set in the top of the wall ahead. *Over to the left is a stone barn and substantial house. This is Cyfanned Fawr.*

2 TURN RIGHT and follow the wall down keeping it to the right to a 'Y' junction. Go down to the right on the more obvious path still with the wall on the right at first. Pass a marker post for the Coastal Path and continue to a stream. Cross this and follow the path down to the left of it. Pass to the right of a ruin as the path veers away from the stream. Enter an area of fine sessile oaks. Go down to a waymarked kissing gate. Pass through this and cross a footbridge. Keep following the obvious path to go through another waymarked kissing gate. Follow the path up to the marker post seen ahead at a path junction. TURN RIGHT down the path that turns into a track to reach a waymarked kissing gate. Pass through this and continue down to a 'T' junction with a level quarry track. TURN LEFT and follow it to the adit that once led to the 'Blue Lake'. *The adit has been blocked by the owner, barring entry to the pool (due to problems with rubbish being dumped there!). The remains of a winding drum are clearly visible on the flat floor of the quarry*

3 There are two options from here. The first is to retrace steps to the 'T' junction and follow the track down to Ffordd Panteinion or much better is to TURN LEFT, with your back to the blocked off adit, to what appears to be a pit and a high stone wall beyond. The wall is in fact the left side of a track. Go easily to this. Note the fine arch to the left. TURN RIGHT down the track to the right of the impressive stone wall to pass through an incline. BEAR RIGHT and descend to a fine high arch to reach a track. TURN LEFT and follow it down to where a zig to left leads to

WALK 11

a kissing gate and finger post. Pass through the gate to Ffordd Panteinion. TURN LEFT back to the layby at the start of the walk.

Cyfanned Fawr *was once quite an important building. It dates from 1748 and in the mid 1900s was the home of Morus Jones, a very well-known poet and winner of many bardic chairs.*

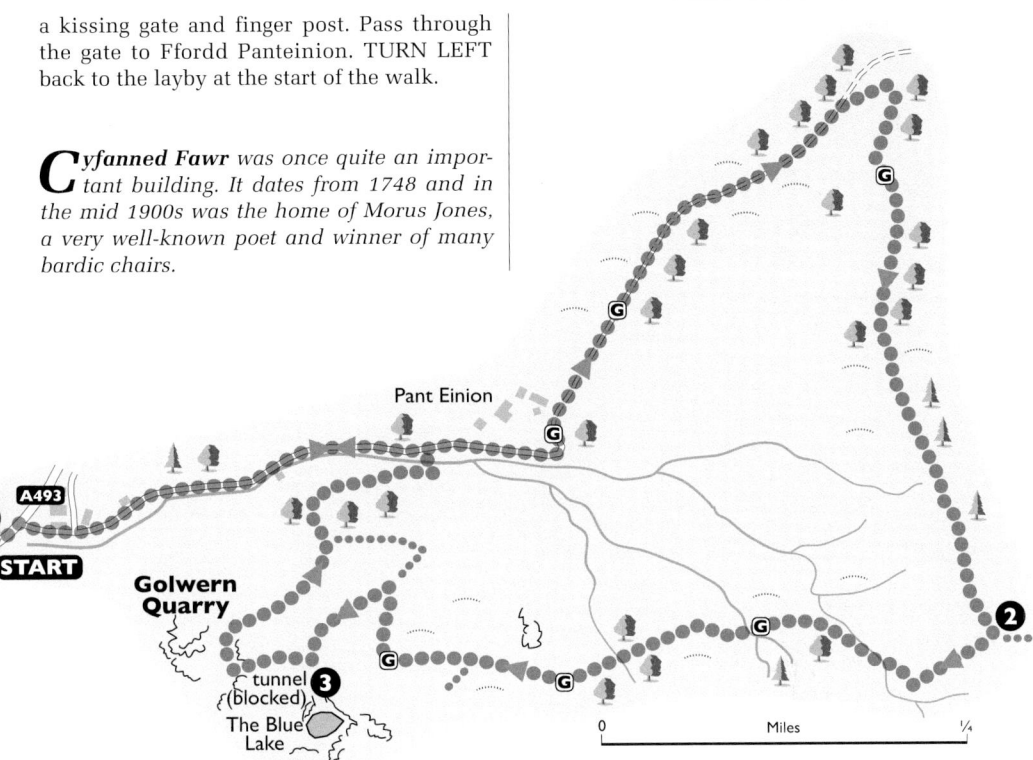

Golwern Quarry *was opened in 1867 and by 1872 was employing 51 men. Slate was brought down the hill on a long incline to the valley road and transported by cart to the ferry at Fairbourne. In the 1890s both Golwern and Henddol quarries operated under one company, Walker and Co. The quarry closed in the late 1920s. Henddol Quarry is found lower down the hillside and was worked between 1865 and 1871. It was reopened in 1883 producing 401 tons of slate against the 50 tons of Golwern in the same year. Forty men were employed producing 10 tons each and at Golwern four men produced around 13 tons per man! When considered with other slate quarries nearby, this was not a great deal. For example the greatest producer of slate, Penrhyn, produced 111,617 tons but with a huge workforce of 2,838 men producing around 38 tons each!*

The 'Blue Lake' *was formed by deliberately filling the quarry pit in 1901. This was undertaken by Arthur McDougal's engineer and was to be used as a reservoir for an ambitious scheme to provide Fairbourne with electric lighting. Most of the pipes were laid but the scheme folded. Arthur McDougal became famous through the manufacture of flour and Fairbourne owes its existence to him. He wanted to create an elite resort, South Barmouth, buying the Ynysfaig Estate and surrounding land in 1895, but his plans never materialised and he sold the estate in 1912. Fairbourne, a singularly inappropriate English name, takes its name from the new railway station he built in 1899. His greatest achievement locally perhaps, was the construction of a horse drawn tramway. This was built originally for construction work but extended to the ferry during 1897 and 1898 and used for transporting tourists in the summer. Subsequently the line became the famous narrow gauge railway.*

WALK 12
AROUND DOROTHEA & CLODDFA'R COED QUARRIES

DESCRIPTION This is a very pleasant and easy 2 mile walk around these two quarries. Although both are flooded there are still many remains of interest, not least Talysarn Hall, the fine and unusual arches close to Dorothea Quarry and the old Cornish beam pump house. The walk is easily followed on tracks and paths and 2 hours gives plenty of time looking around the remains.

START At the end of the dead end road in Talysarn.

DIRECTIONS Turn off the A487 Porthmadog to Caernarfon road into Penegroes. Turn on to the B4418 that leads over to Rhyd Ddu. Continue into Talysarn. At the 'T' junction where the B4418 turns 90 degrees to the right, turn left. The village Community Hall and large car park is on the left. Turn right after 100 yards and follow the village road over several humps to where there is a dead end sign and a road bears up to the left. Continue into the dead end road and park near the roundabout at the end.

1 Follow the level track leading off directly ahead at the roundabout. Ignoring a track going up to the left continue for 200 yards to a substantial barrier. Pass this through the kissing gate to the left. It is possible to turn left on a path 10 yards further to view the flooded pit of Talysarn Quarry. Return to the track and turn left. Continue to go through the gateway for the old Talysarn Hall. *The flooded Dorothea Quarry can be seen to the right.* Keep following the track ignoring all turnings to the track side ruins of the Hall. The track rises slightly here and continues to a fine vantage point overlooking Dorothea Quarry. *The flooded workings are 550 feet deep and it appears that it is a single pit.* Descend slightly and go past a turning/parking area. Go up a short rise to a track junction at the top. Keep straight ahead and descend 50 yards to where a muddy track goes acutely right. Follow this as it passes between high walls to pass below two interesting arches. Bear left and walk through two tunnels below inclines. Bear right to a track and turn left along it to reach a 'Y' junction.

2 Follow the track that bears right and continue to where it descends slightly to the Cornish beam pump house on the left. A short ascent leads up to another fine vantage point of Dorothea Quarry with Mynydd Mawr 2,290 feet beyond it. Continue along the track and descend to the main track coming from Talysarn. TURN LEFT along it to where and old redundant metal kissing gate is seen to the left 150 yards further. TURN LEFT and pass to the left of it. Follow the clear path past two seats to where it descends almost to the quarry pool. *There is a great view along here of Talysarn and the flooded Cloddfa'r Coed Quarry.* Cross a footbridge and follow the path as it rises gently to a gate. Immediately after passing through is a 'Y' junction. Follow the right arm to reach a 'T' junction. TURN RIGHT and continue to reach a kissing gate. Pass through this and TURN RIGHT to go up the access track to reach the roundabout at the start of the walk and car.

*T*alysarn *was once a hive of industry. Nowadays it is a peaceful little village. Two famous people lived here Robert Williams Parry 1884 – 1956 an influential Welsh poet and the Reverend John Jones 1796 – 1857 one of the most influential Methodists of his age. Talysarn Quarry opened in 1798 and became the fourth largest producer of slate in the Nantlle Valley. In 1882 it produced 8,210 tons. The village began developing in the late 18th century. Cloddfa'r Coed Quarry was one of the main quarries in the district between 1850 and 1870. Dorothea Quarry opened in 1820 and very quickly became the dominant undertaking in the area. In 1848 records show that 200 men produced 5,000 tons per annum but by 1882 some 533 men were employed when production rose to 16,598 tons per annum. In total there were six pits. In 1906 the Cornish*

WALK 12

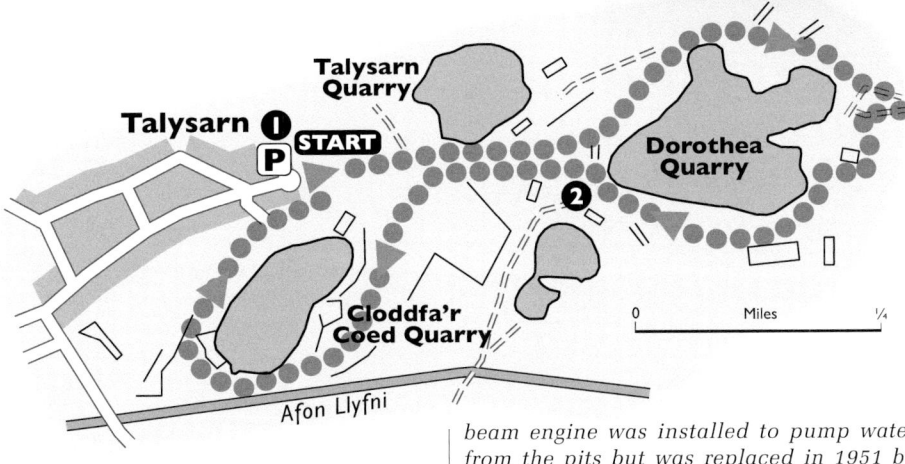

beam engine was installed to pump water from the pits but was replaced in 1951 by electric pumps. The quarry closed in 1968.

Tramway Tunnel at Dorothea Quarry

WALK 13
TALYSARN, DOROTHEA, PEN YR ORSEDD & CILGWYN QUARRIES

DESCRIPTION This is a fine 5¼ mile walk taking in the quarries of the Talysarn and Nantlle areas. There are some magnificent views of the whole of the Nantlle Ridge as well as Mynydd Mawr 2,290 feet. The walk is easily followed on tracks, roads and paths and 3 hours gives plenty of looking around time.

START At the end of the dead end road in Talysarn.

DIRECTIONS Turn off the A487 Porthmadog to Caernarfon road into Penegroes. Turn on to the B4418 that leads over to Rhyd Ddu. Continue into Talysarn. At the 'T' junction where the B4418 turns 90° to the right, turn left. The village Community Hall and large car park is on the left. Turn right after 100 yards and follow the village road over several humps to where there is a dead end sign and a road bears up to the left. Continue into the dead end road and park near the roundabout at the end.

1 Follow the level track leading off directly ahead at the roundabout. Ignoring a track going up to the left continue for 200 yards to a substantial barrier. Pass this through the kissing gate to the left. It is possible to turn left on a path 10 yards further to view the flooded pit of Talysarn Quarry. Return to the track and turn left. Continue to go through the gateway for the old Talysarn Hall. *The flooded Dorothea Quarry can be seen to the right.* Keep following the track ignoring all turnings to the track side ruins of the Hall. The track rises slightly here and continues to a fine vantage point overlooking Dorothea Quarry. *The flooded workings are 550 feet deep.* Descend slightly and pass a turning/parking area. Keep following the main track ahead ignoring all junctions to the left and right to pass below two fine slate buttresses to reach a tarmac road close to a large house, Bryn Deulyn. Follow the road to the B4418.

2 TURN LEFT along this. Pass a phone box and cross a footbridge. TURN LEFT at the finger post 10 yards further through an old kissing gate. Follow the path up to the right of the spoil heap of Pen yr Orsedd quarry with an old slate and wire fence to the left. When this goes down to the left go up right close to the gorse bushes to where there is a fine view of Mynydd Mawr. Keep following the path along a grassy shelf to reach a ladder stile 50 yards left of some ruins. *There is a terrific view of the Nantlle Ridge from here. Left to right these are Y Garn 2,077 feet, Mynydd Drws-y-coed 2,280 feet, Trum y Ddysgl 2,362 feet, Mynydd Tal-y-mignedd 2,142 feet and Craig Cwm Silyn 2,408 feet.* Climb over and continue straight ahead passing to the left of gorse bushes to climb over another ladder stile. Bear very slightly left across the field to go through a kissing gate to the left of a gate.

3 TURN LEFT up the track and pass through another kissing gate 7 yards ahead. Follow the track up to reach a 'Y' junction. TURN LEFT. Continue to a gate with a fine old metal stile to the right. Pass through the gate and cross the stream. Bear left up the track and continue through ruins. The track keeps rising to where it levels and swings left to reach a track 'T' junction. Continue along the level track to a gate with a kissing gate to the left. Pass through this to a narrow tarmac road. Follow this up into Fron. At the road junction TURN LEFT to the cross roads in the village by a phone box.

4 TURN LEFT down Tai Bryn Twrog following the tarmac road to where it ends. Continue straight ahead on the track still with magnificent views of the Nantlle Ridge. Cross straight over a track junction and continue straight ahead to reach a wall. *A recommended optional ascent of Mynydd y Cilgwyn can be made by turning right 50 yards before the wall on a narrow but clearly seen and followed path that wanders gradually up from here up to reach the 1,138 feet*

WALK 13

summit. There is a circle of stones that can be entered via 'paved block' entrance to the central small cairn. The summit is a fine viewpoint where the Nantlle Ridge is dominant, Llyn Nantlle, Mynydd Mawr, the village of Fron, Moel Tryfan 1,401 feet beyond it and further beyond still is Moel Eilio 2,382 feet. From the far side of the circle opposite the entrance TURN LEFT on a path that heads down to the easily seen road in Cilgwyn close to the phone box. If this option is not taken continue along the walled track past an information panel above Gloddfa Glytiau Quarry. Continue above the now filled in Cilgwyn Quarry into Cilgwyn. There is a finger post on the right with an obvious path going up Mynydd y Cilgwyn to the right.

5 At the 'Y' junction by the phone box TURN LEFT and pas a way marker on a telegraph pole. Continue down to a road junction coming up from the left. There is a finger post at the far side. TURN LEFT and 50 yards further

TURN RIGHT down a path to pass through a short tunnel to reach a track. TURN LEFT and immediately go through a waymarked kissing gate to the right of gate. Follow the track to the right at the 'Y' junction ahead and continue down this to a kissing gate on the right at the apex of the left hand bend. Pass through this. There is a way marker for the Pilgrims Way here. Follow the walled grassy track down to where it opens out by a ruin and marker post. Go down steps on the right and through an old waymarked kissing gate. Continue down through another walled section and through yet another kissing gate. Keep going down past a marker post to go through another kissing gate. Descend more steps. Continue to more steps and descend these to go through a waymarked gate. Go straight ahead to join a track and TURN LEFT down it. Pass through the gate at bottom by the finger post to join the track of the outward walk. TURN RIGHT and follow it back into Talysarn.

*T*alysarn was once a hive of industry. Nowadays it is a peaceful little village. Two famous people lived here Robert Williams Parry 1884–1956 an influential Welsh poet and the Reverend John Jones 1796–1857 one of the most influential Methodists of his age. Talysarn Quarry opened in 1798 and became the fourth largest producer of slate in the Nantlle Valley. In 1882 it produced 8,210 tons. The village began developing in the late 18th century. Cloddfa'r Coed Quarry was one of the main quarries in the district between 1850 and 1870. Dorothea Quarry opened in 1820 and very quickly became the dominant undertaking in the area. In 1848 records show that 200 men produced 5,000 tons per annum but by 1882 some 533 men were employed when production rose to 16,598 tons per annum. In total there were six pits. In 1906 the Cornish beam engine was installed to pump water from the pits but was replaced in 1951 by electric pumps. The quarry closed in 1968.

WALK 14
MOEL TRYFAN QUARRY & ASSCOCIATED QUARRIES

DESCRIPTION This is a great 3½ mile walk with amazing views not only of the Nantlle Ridge but an unusual view of Snowdon and some of its satellite peaks. There are many remains to be seen and the walk is easy to follow on tracks, paths and roads. The summit of Moel Tryfan 1,401 feet is unusual and a geological phenomenon. Well worth a visit in its own right for the terrific views. There is an alternative way back to Fron from the summit that shortens the walk by ½ mile This avoids a ½ mile road section. Allow 2 hours for the longer walk and 1¾ for the shorter.

START Close to the cross roads in Fron.

DIRECTIONS Turn off the A487 at the signs for Groeslon and follow directions to Carmel and Fron. At the cross roads in the tiny village turn left towards Rhosgadfan and park almost immediately to the right or left in non-tarmacked laybys.

1 From the layby on the right TURN RIGHT up the track and pass a finger post indicating the way to Waunfawr is 4 miles. Follow the rough track up to where it turns 90 degrees to the left. Continue straight ahead on the less well defined track. It looks like there is no way forward at the end of this but a cleverly concealed and pretty fenced path goes up above the flooded pit of Braich Quarry towards the white houses that are seen up ahead. *There is a great view of the Nantlle Ridge over to the right – Mynydd Mawr 2,290 feet is dominant straight ahead.* The path widens as the houses are approached and continues to the left of them. Ruins above Braich Quarry are clearly visible. The path becomes a track and bears left to a wall and small cottages. Leave the track and bear left at the end of these keeping the wall to the left. *There is a great view of Anglesey and Holy Mountain from here.* Continue to a kissing gate.

2 Pass through this and follow the path with a fence to the left. At the junction with a major quarry track cross straight over it and follow the less well defined track going uphill to where it bends 90 degrees to the right. Continue straight ahead up another track towards a fence. When this bears right go left to join another track at the fence corner. TURN RIGHT and continue up more steeply to reach a fence. Beyond this is a quarry track, beyond which are the spoil heaps of Moel Tryfan Quarry. Keeping the fence to the left continue up to a huge quarry on the left. *This is Alexandra Quarry.* The path levels somewhat here. Still keeping the fence to the left Snowdon 3,560 feet and Crib y Ddysgl 3,494 feet come in to view after a very short rise and short descent to a track. TURN LEFT along it and continue through ruins again with the fence to the left. Where the fence ends bear left then go right up to a level track. TURN LEFT along this until a poorly defined track goes off to the left. There are short walls to the right.

3 TURN LEFT. There is a line of stones across the track 5 yards up it. After 10 yards the track becomes a path bearing right and up past a ruin. Continue up with a short steep section to reach the summit of Moel Tryfan. An information plaque on the summit details the importance of this site. *There is an outstanding panoramic view from the summit and takes in Snowdon, Mynydd Mawr, all of the Nantlle Ridge, Yr Eifl (The Rivals) on the Llyn Peninsula, Anglesey and Caernarfon and Moel Eilo 2,382 feet.* From the summit follow the path down in a north westerly direction. It becomes steep and reaches a track at a covered reservoir. Follow the track for 100 yards to a cross roads.

4 TURN LEFT. Follow the track through a walled section and above houses. The track continues to a sharp right hand hairpin bend to reach a tarmac road. TURN LEFT at the finger post and follow the track past ruins to a gate before a house. Go up to the left and pass above it keeping to the left

WALK 14

of the boundary fence to reach a gate. Pass through this and immediately turn right on a courtesy path. Follow this around fields to a gate. Go through this and continue ahead to a wide dusty track. TURN RIGHT down this to reach the road. TURN LEFT up this back into Fron.

The summit rocks of Moel Tryfan were deposited during the Ice Age 20 to 30,000 years ago because the glacial Irish Sea was in conflict with the mainland Welsh ice. Sand and gravel from the sea along with shells and wood were dredged from the seabed by the marine ice and thrust southwards to be deposited on the summit of Moel Tryfan. Today the summit still plays and important part in the development of Glacial Theories and Pleistocene studies.

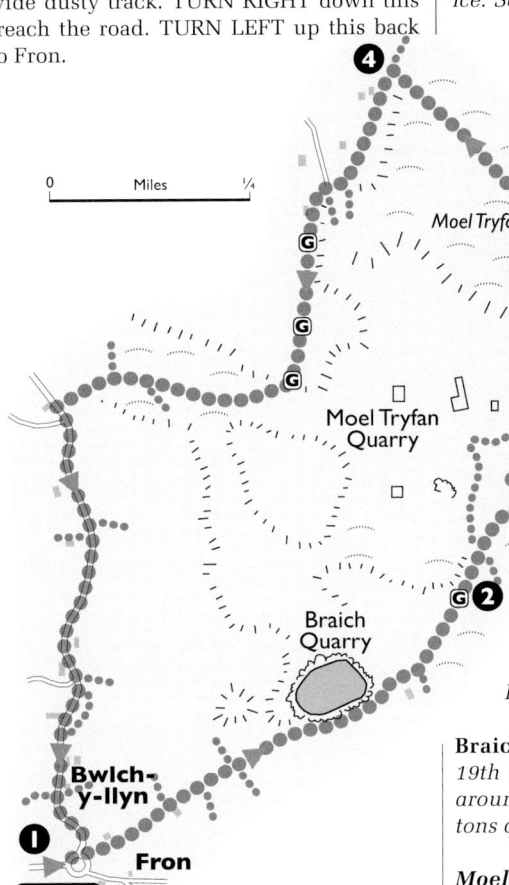

Braich Quarry was developed in the early 19th century and became an important site around 1868. In 1882 its output was 2,614 tons quarried by 124 men. It closed in 1911.

Moel Tryfan Quarry expanded quickly in the 1880s, bucking the trend of those days, having been connected to the North Wales Narrow Gauge Railway. It employed some 200 men. There are five layers of spoil heaps. The upper ones had 6 feet high storm walls to prevent the wagons from becoming airborne! How strong does the wind get up there? Small scale working continues today.

Alexandra Quarry opened in the 1860s and at its height produced 6,000 tons when it employed 200 men. The mills closed in the late 1930s although small scale quarrying takes place today.

ALTERNATIVE RETURN FROM THE SUMMIT

Follow the obvious path heading roughly south towards the spoil heaps and Fron to where a very short but steep descent leads to a quarry track. TURN RIGHT down this and descend to a barrier. Pass around this to the right and at the 'T' junction TURN LEFT ignoring the barrier to the right. Follow the track to where it was crossed over on the outward walk. TURN RIGHT to return into Fron as for the outward walk.

WALK 15
TY MAWR, YNYSYPANDY SLATE MILL

DESCRIPTION This is an easy 2¼ mile walk visiting an iconic but ruined slate mill. The views across Llyn Cwmystradllyn are lovely with the Gorseddau Quarry clearly visible at the far end of the lake. The huge bulk of Moel Hebog 2,569 feet towers above over to the left. Although the walk only takes 1¼ hours allow another 30 minutes to fully explore the mill and its surroundings. The valley road is very quiet and the walk is very easily followed on paths, tracks and roads.

START At the car park by the dam in Cwmystradllyn.

DIRECTIONS Turn off the A487 for the signs to Golan. From the roundabout in the centre of Portmadog it is 2½ miles when heading towards Caernarfon whilst it is 2¼ miles past the turning for the B4417 when coming from the Caernarfon direction. Follow signs towards

1 From the car park TURN RIGHT through the gate and follow the tarmac road across the dam. *There is a great view of Gorseddau Quarry and Moel Hebog along here.* At the far side BEAR RIGHT to where a track starts at the end of the tarmac. Follow this down to a ladder stile on the left. Climb over this and BEAR RIGHT across a short damp bit. A drier path continues and passes through some boulders. There is a marker post up to the left. Pass through a gap in a low wall and continue with a low wall to the left to reach a gate with a ladder stile to the right. Climb over this and cross the field towards the obvious gate to reach a track. DO NOT go through the gate but TURN RIGHT along the track.

2 Follow the track to Ynys Wen farm. Pass through a waymarked gate and continue through the farm to its access track. Follow the track and pass through a gate to the right of a cattle grid. Continue past Ereiniog Farm and down to a junction with the valley road by a phone box. *There are superb views of the mill along this stretch of road.* TURN RIGHT and RIGHT again 50 yards further before crossing the bridge over the Afon Henwy through an old metal kissing gate, signed for the mill. Follow the path up to the mill.

3 Facing the mill entrance turn up to the left up the left hand side of the building to the higher tramway. TURN LEFT along it and follow it as it curves leftwards to where there is an obvious gate on the right. TURN RIGHT through a gap in the fence then TURN LEFT by the gate. (Passing through this leads to the road previously walked down). Keeping to the right of the fence and with the tram road wall to the right continue to a ladder stile. Climb over this and still follow the tram road to pass through a gate guarding a footbridge. Cross the bridge that spans the Afon Henwy. The tram road continues damply and boulder filled. Avoid this by continuing above and to the right to climb over two ladder stiles in quick succession. The next ladder stile at the start of a conifer plantation is defunct and is easily passed to the right. Continue with the conifers on the right and fence to the left to reach a stile. Climb over this to the road. TURN RIGHT and follow it back to the car park. Just before reaching it at the 90° bend there is a café at Tyddyn Mawr. Fishing permits may also be obtained here.

T*he very impressive* Ty Mawr slate processing mill is possibly unique in that it has three floors. The mill was built between 1855 and 1857 by Robert Gill and John Harris who formed the 'Bangor and Porthmadoc Slate and Slab Company Ltd.'. Roofing slates for the mill were made at the quarry although the majority of slate produced there was slab and was processed in the mill. Normally mills are long and single story but here a 'vertical' process was undertaken. The machine room was built regardless of the cost and had a large number of sawing, planing and dressing machines. The range of products was quite astonishing – flooring slabs and window sills. Slab slate

WALK 15

was used to make cisterns, tanks, wine coolers, bread, pickling, pig feeding troughs, urinals, filters, head and foot stones for graves, tombs, monuments, clock faces and sundials. It will be seen that there is very little waste which shows that there was not much produced in the 10 years or so of the operation of the mill. The mill and quarry closed in 1871. It is thought that the mill was used afterwards as a chapel whilst in 1888 an Eisteddfod was held here. The wooden floors were taken out in the 1890s and the roof removed in 1906 along with the iron framed windows.

The design of the mill was probably drawn up by James Brunlees. Slate was brought in on two levels, the upper and middle storey. Inside there is an impressive wheel pit that housed a 26 feet diameter overshot waterwheel.

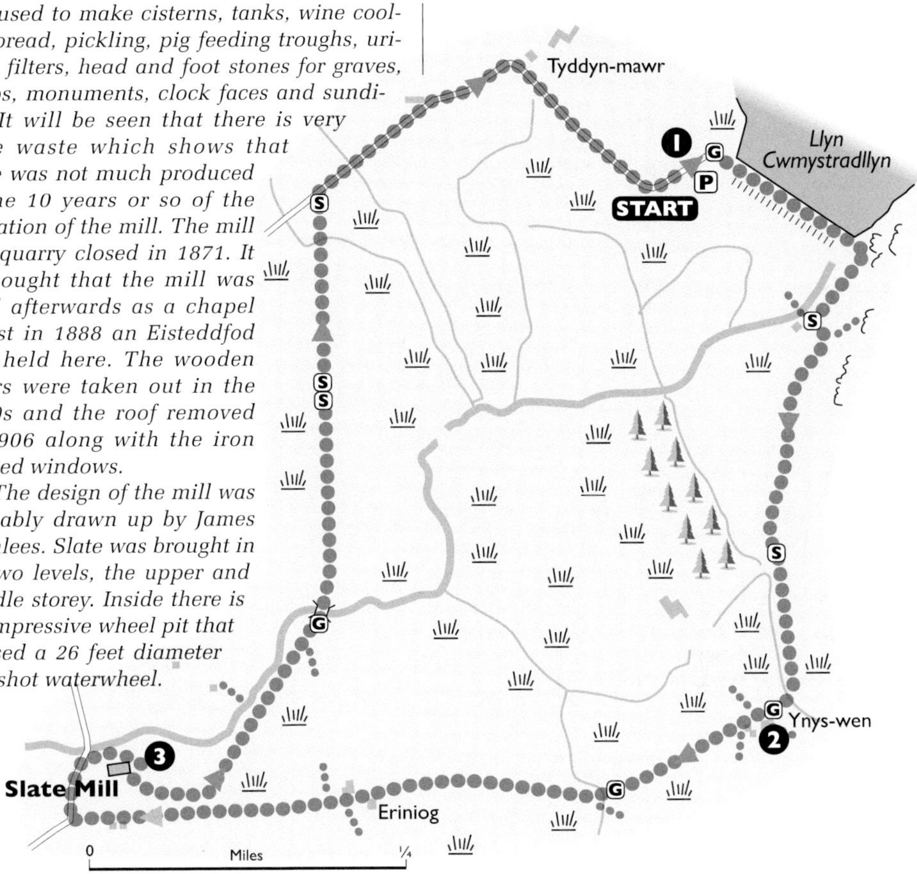

A quote in local paper at the time epitomises the blind optimism of these Victorian entrepreneurs – 'everything that could facilitate the works was produced, nothing being wanted but the slate vein'.

Ty Mawr Slate Mill

WALK 16
GORSEDDAU QUARRY

DESCRIPTION This is one of two walks to the quarry and is very gently rising, as to be seemingly level. It is an easy 3½ mile walk in fine surroundings. The views of Moel Hebog, 2,569 feet, are outstanding. Although the walk does not visit the abandoned and ruined Treforys village it is still a great walk. There are some grand remains at the quarry not least the stunning overhanging wall built to hold back a rather large spoil heap. Allow 2 hours. This gives plenty of time to explore.
START At the car park by the dam in Cwmystradllyn.
DIRECTIONS Turn off the A487 for the signs to Golan. From the roundabout in the centre of Portmadog it is 2½ miles when heading towards Caernarfon whilst it is 2¼ miles past the turning for the B4417 when coming from the Caernarfon direction. Follow signs towards Cwmystradllyn.

1 From the car park TURN LEFT and walk back along the road to a junction with a track on the right where the road bends 90 degrees to the left. On the right is Tyddyn Mawr with a great tea room. Fishing permits can be obtained here. TURN RIGHT as indicated by a finger post just beyond the house along the left hand of two tracks. Pass through a gate and continue to reach and go over a ladder stile to the right of a padlocked gate. The track becomes much rougher and continues past some ruins, the remains of Tal-y-llyn Farm. Opposite the last ruin is a 'Y' junction of tracks. IGNORE the one going up to the left. Keep following the level track to go through a gate. There is a ladder stile to the left. Gorseddau Quarry is now very prominent ahead. The track continues to another gate with ladder stile to the right.

2 Climb over this. Continue and pass through a gate just to the right of the ruined sheds. Continue through a coppice and leave it through a gate just after crossing a stream. (This is often open). *The large mound of stones to the left of the track in the coppice is all that remains of the Quarry Managers house – it eventually became a youth hostel.* Follow the tramway to a gate just before the large spoil heap and a remarkably built overhanging wall. Pass below this marvelling at its construction then go up very slightly to a ruin. Continue through a gap in the wall to the base of the incline. Return from here but instead of passing above the ruin pass below for a fine view of it and of Moel Hebog. Continue back to the car park as for the outward walk, stopping for a cuppa at Tyddyn Mawr.

WALK 16

When the quarry first opened in 1807 it was a tiny concern, although it very gradually grew in size. In the North Wales Chronicle of April 1836 it was mentioned as being offered for sale. After many changes of hands the lease was bought by a Bavarian, Henry Tobias von Uster, a mining engineer, in 1853. Robert Gill and John Harris took over the lease in 1854, and formed the 'Bangor and Porthmadoc Slate and Slab Company Ltd', although Uster maintained his interest in the quarry for its lifetime. Apart from Ty Mawr, the quarry mill, being built between 1855 and 1857, other parts of the infrastructure were completed at this time and over £50,000 was spent. This included the agent's house, a village, Treforys, for the workforce and connecting the quarry by the 3 foot gauge Gorseddau Tramway railway that lead to Porthmadog. Output grew very slowly from 226 tons in 1857 to 1859 when 200 men produced fewer than 1,400 tons. My maths indicates that equates to around 7 tons per man! In 1860 at the peak of production 2,148 tons of slate was produced. A steady decline then started until in 1865 only 860 tons were produced down to a meagre 25 tons in 1867. This led to the liquidation of the company in 1871.

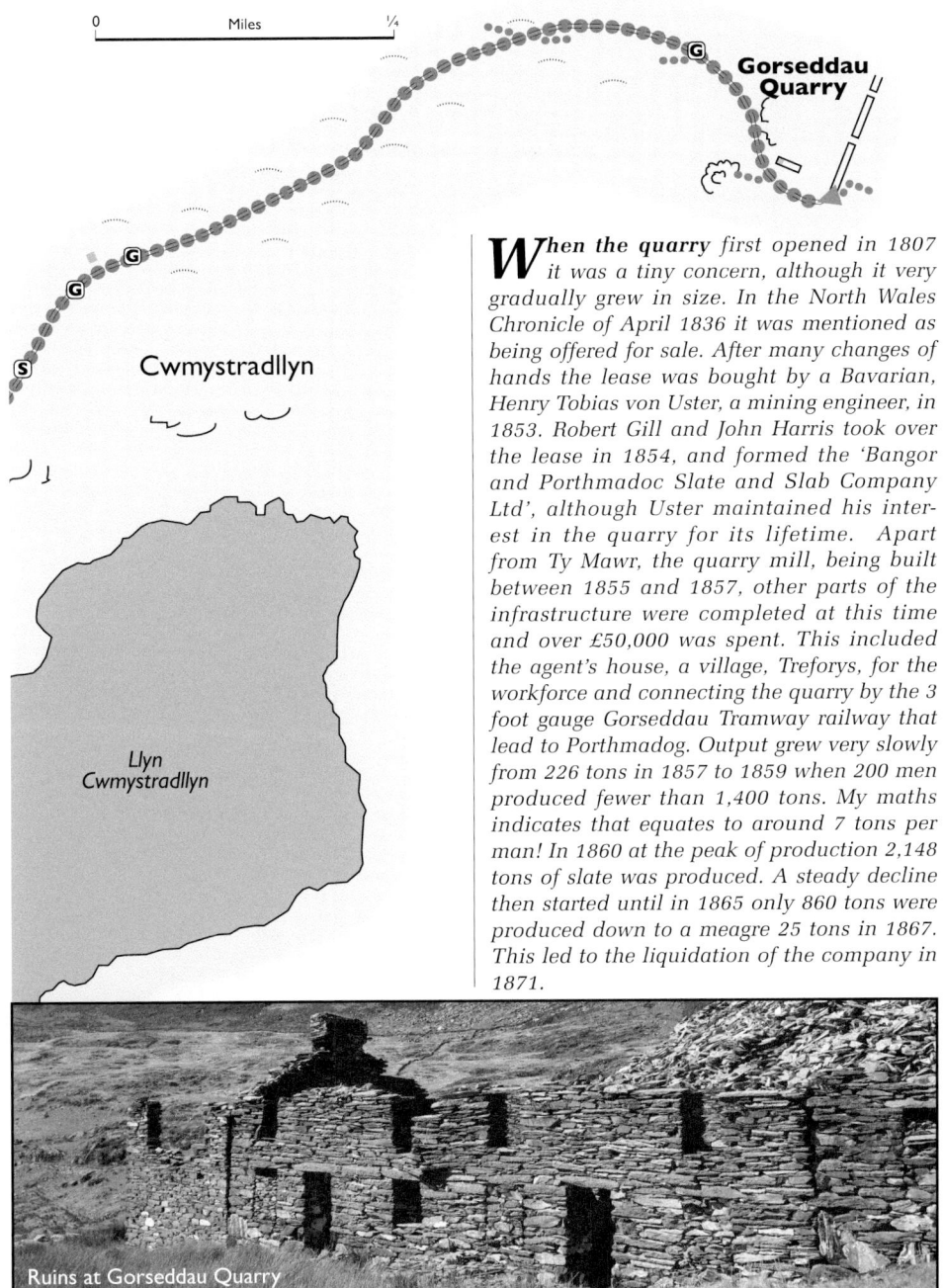

Ruins at Gorseddau Quarry

WALK 17

THE RUINED VILLAGE OF TREFORYS, & GORSEDDAU QUARRY

DESCRIPTION This the second of two walks to the quarry visits the long abandoned village of Treforys before continuing to to Gorseddau Quarry. The section from the village to the quarry is quite boggy in parts The 3½ mile walk makes one think of all the people who once lived and worked in the remote spot. Views of Moel Hebog, 2,569 feet, are outstanding. There are some grand remains at the quarry not least the stunning overhanging wall built to hold back a spoil heap. Allow 2¾ hours. This gives plenty of time to explore.

START At the car park by the dam in Cwmystradllyn.

DIRECTIONS Turn off the A487 for the signs to Golan. From the roundabout in the centre of Portmadog it is 2½ miles when heading towards Caernarfon whilst it is 2¼ miles past the turning for the B4417 when coming from the Caernarfon direction. Follow signs towards Cwmystradllyn.

1 From the car park TURN LEFT and walk back along the road to a junction with a track on the right where the road bends 90 degrees to the left. On the right here is Tyddyn Mawr with a great tea room. Fishing permits can be obtained here. TURN RIGHT as indicated by a finger post just beyond the house along a track. Pass through a gate and continue to reach and go over a ladder stile to the right of a padlocked gate. The track becomes much rougher and continues past some ruins, the remains of Tal-y-llyn Farm. Opposite the last ruin is a 'Y' junction of tracks. Go up the left arm of the 'Y' to reach a padlocked gate. This is unfastened by releasing a shackle. PLEASE REPLACE SECURELY. Continue up with the wall to the right to a ladder stile. Climb over this to the desolate ruins of the Treforys Village immediately over to the left.

2 Follow the less clear track and cross the stream by a wall corner. Continue straight ahead below the ruins. There is a great view of Gorseddau Quarry over to the right and Moel Hebog up to the left. Follow an intermittent grass shelf to reach and go over a ladder stile. Continue straight ahead keeping a low wall to the right Follow the wall down all the way to the Gorseddau tramway. TURN LEFT along it and follow it to reach a gate. Go through this to pass below an amazing stone built overhanging wall. This was built to hold back the spoil heap! At the 'Y' junction bear left and up and pass above a ruin to reach an incline.

3 To start the return walk pass below the ruin for a fine view of it and Moel Hebog and re-join the tramway. Pass through the gate by the overhanging wall and continue to a gate immediately before entering a coppice. Pass through the gate (sometimes left open) and cross a stream. *Up to the right is a mound of stones. It is all that remains of the Quarry Managers house that eventually*

WALK 17

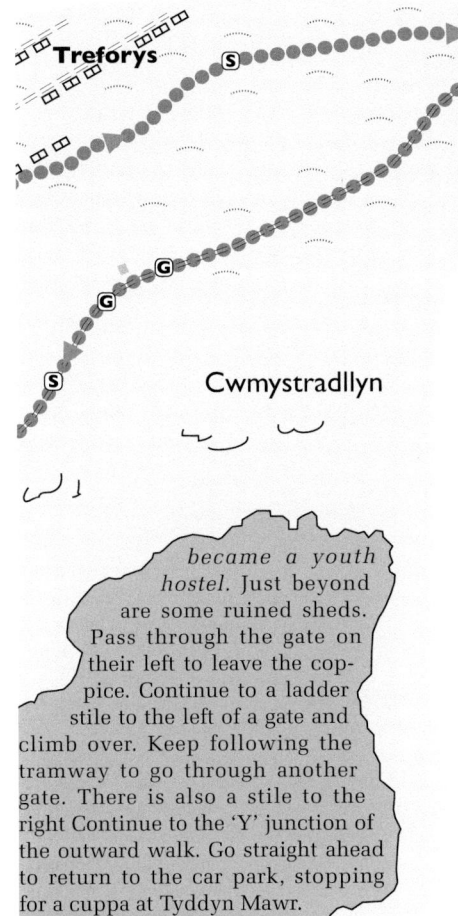

When the quarry first opened in 1807 it was a tiny concern, although it very gradually grew in size. In the North Wales Chronicle of April 1836 it was mentioned as being offered for sale. After many changes of hands the lease was bought by a Bavarian, Henry Tobias von Uster, a mining engineer, in 1853. Robert Gill and John Harris took over the lease in 1854, and formed the 'Bangor and Porthmadoc Slate and Slab Company Ltd', although Uster maintained his interest in the quarry for its lifetime. Apart from Ty Mawr, the quarry mill, being built between 1855 and 1857, other parts of the infrastructure were completed at this time and over £50,000 was spent. This included the agent's house, a village, Treforys, for the workforce and connecting the quarry by the 3 foot gauge Gorseddau Tramway railway that lead to Porthmadog. Output grew very slowly from 226 tons in 1857 to 1859 when 200 men produced fewer than 1,400 tons. My maths indicates that equates to around 7 tons per man! In 1860 at the peak of production 2,148 tons of slate was produced. A steady decline then started until in 1865 only 860 tons were produced down to a meagre 25 tons in 1867. This led to the liquidation of the company in 1871.

*T*reforys, the abandoned quarry workers village overlooking Llyn Cwmystradllyn, was built in 1857 and comprised 36 houses in three streets. It was named after the landowner, Robert Morris Griffiths of Bangor. Each house had a quarter acre of ground in which they were able, with difficulty due to the acidic and peaty ground, to supplement their wages from the quarry by growing root crops and keeping a few animals such as pigs, cows or sheep. In the 1861 census it was recorded that nine families lived there and the total of people living there were 18 adults and 27 children. At the 1871 census the whole village was regarded as unoccupied! Plas Llyn the Quarry Managers House was still occupied in 1871 but by 1878 this too was unoccupied. At the turn of the century Plas Llyn became a fishing lodge and for a few years after 1949 it was a Youth Hostel. Now alas it is just a pile of stones.

WALK 18
PRINCE OF WALES QUARRY

DESCRIPTION This 2½ mile walk is full of interest with many surface features. For such an unproductive mine there is much to see. As such the walk will occupy 2 hours or more to fully explore the area. There are some lovely views and in spring time the start of the walk is a carpet of bluebells. The views are dramatic especially when passing by the reservoir with the looming high and vertiginous grassy cliffs of Moel Lefn 2,093 feet on the right soaring skyward. Views across the valley on the left to the Nantlle Ridge in particular are lovely. On the left is the serrated ridge leading to the summit of Craig Cwm Silyn 2,408 feet whilst to the right is Trum y Ddysgl 2,326 feet and right again Drws y Coed 2,280 feet.

START The dedicated car park at the end of the tarmac road at the head of Cwm Pennant.

DIRECTIONS Follow the A487 Porthmadog to Caernarfon road from either the south or north to the turning for Cwm Pennant. Follow this very quiet minor road to the car parking area at the end of the tarmac. A small fee is payable at the farm near the head of the valley. There are picnic tables here.

1 Climb over the ladder stile on the left of the car park and cross the clapper bridge to a stile sporting a Private notice asking people to keep to the path. Climb over the stile and keeping the fence and stream to the right continue to where the path quickly veers left away from the fence. Climb steadily to a marker post. This whole area is a carpet of bluebells in spring time. Keep bearing left to reach a marker post by a clump of gorse bushes. Continue up to the left of these to another marker post below ruins. Pass below them and go up to reach a ladder stile.

2 Climb over this and go right to a 'Y' junction. Follow the right arm of the 'Y' and continue around to a ruin. *This has some fine arched stonework and was the mill.* Pass through this. Continue noting the launder pillars to the right. *These supported a water trough for the mill.* BEAR RIGHT on the clear path, with a stream to the right, going gradually up. There are some pretty large boulders in the streambed to the right and the huge brooding cliffs of Moel Lefn towering above give an air of foreboding. Pass to the left of the dam wall. *Note that there are two walls. The gap in between them would have been filled with clay and allowed for the dam to be heightened at some stage.*

3 Follow the path alongside the reservoir and continue straight ahead at the far end to arrive at a wall end. *Looking back the remains of a drum house will be seen silhouetted on the skyline.* There are ruins to the right. BEAR RIGHT and pass above and to the left end of these. Continue up to the right hand end of a level. BEAR RIGHT slightly and pass to the right of a small spoil heap with a wall to the right and go up to the next level. Keep going up and pass to the right of three confers to reach the next level. There is a mine entrance on the right. DO NOT ENTER. Continue up and pass to the right of another small heap and pass above the mine entrance to arrive at a large level area and a deep pit. Another path joins here to become one path. Follow this up to the right to reach a wall with a gate. DO NOT go through. *There is great view of Trum y Ddysgl and Mynydd Drws-y-coed from here. If desired and to make a longer walk it is possible to ascend Trum y Ddysgl up the broad grassy rib. It is a steep and tedious ascent.*

4 Return to the level area and junction of paths. Continue ahead past the obvious ruined huts, the barracks where the workers stayed, on the level path and descend with a high wall to the right to more ruins. These are called Waliau where slate was hand trimmed and dressed. Keeping these to the left continue to where the path descends to more ruins. Follow the path down on the left of the incline to the next level. Walk down the incline to where a narrow but obvious path breaks off to the right half way down. Continue along the broad grassy ridge to where the path passes to the right and below a grassy knoll. The path descends gradually

WALK 18

until above the ruins to the right passed earlier in the walk. *There is a grand view down to the left of the mill from here.* A short steep descent leads to the ladder stile crossed earlier. Return to the car park retracing steps of the outward walk.

The Prince of Wales Quarry was developed in the 1860s, although not very productively until 1873 when production greatly increased. Seven levels were developed. The fine mill was built at the terminus of the Gorseddau Tramway and was powered by water. Having the tramway meant that there was no longer any need for the slate to be carted over Bwlch-y-Ddwy-elor to Cwm Gwyfrai. At its peak the mine employed around 200 men who produced 5,000 tons annually. It closed in 1886 but was spasmodically worked until 1920. All the roofing slates were split on the terraces or levels. The mill only dealt with slab.

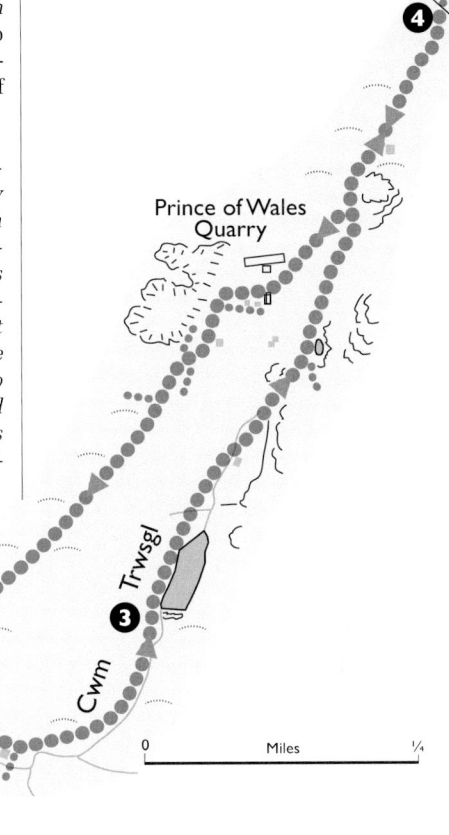

The mill for the Prince of Wales Mine

WALK 19
BRYN EGLWYS QUARRY

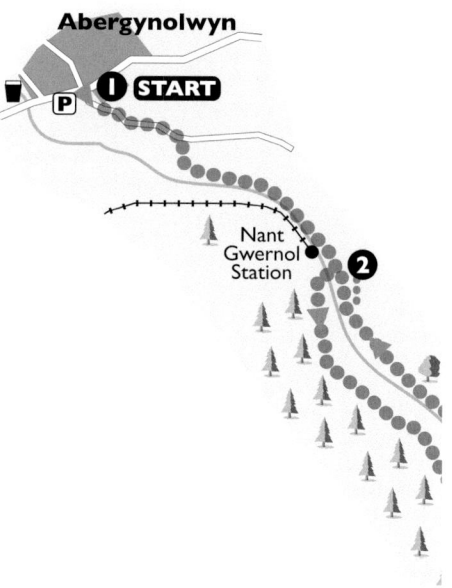

DESCRIPTION Starting in beautiful woodland, enhanced by a tumbling stream, this great 4 mile walk arrives at the old quarry workings and explores the production area. On the return leg the huge deep hole of an extraction quarry is passed. The final part of the walk through the pretty woodland once more is a fitting end to this walk. Allow 2¾ hours.

START At the Post Office/Community Centre/Café car park in the middle of Abergynolwyn.

DIRECTIONS From Tywyn take the A493 Dolgellau road as far as Bryncrug. Turn right here on to the B4405 signed Talyllyn. At Abergynolwyn turn right at the cross roads almost opposite the Railway Inn into the car park. Coming from the north turn off the A487 at Minffordd onto the B4405 and follow it to Abergynolwyn and turn left into the car park.

1 Walk up the road past the community centre. This quickly becomes very steep and continues up to a finger post on the right. TURN RIGHT here and follow the gentle path above to reach a 'Y' junction. Go up to the left and continue easily still above the tumbling and cascading Nant Gwernol to a short gentle rise. At the top of this TURN RIGHT across the footbridge and follow the fenced path to Nant Gwernol Station.

2 Just before the platform TURN LEFT up the steps to go a steep path, the old Alltwyllt incline. A long flight of steps is reached and climbed. At the top of these the path turns acutely right and continues to a path junction. TURN LEFT (right goes to Abergynolwyn station) and go up to the top of the Alltwyllt incline. *Note the twin lines and the old braking mechanism hereabouts.* Easy level walking follows the tramway to a footbridge down to the left. IGNORE this. Continue straight ahead on a path that rises steadily with the Nant Moelfre on the left to arrive at a footbridge. TURN LEFT over this and continue up to reach a track at a 'Y' junction. TURN LEFT then follow the right arm of the 'Y'. *The rounded form of Tarren y Gesail 2,188 feet is across to the left.* Continue along the track to a marker post on the left. There is a monkey puzzle tree 50 yards ahead on the right.

3 TURN RIGHT up the grassy Cwmcwm incline. *There is a 'wind up' story machine here, just after starting up!* At the top bear left where a marker post is seen to the right. Continue along the obvious path part of the original tramway to the remains of a drum house in the conifers. The path descends through spoil heaps to reach a fence. Pass the information panel and another 'wind up' story machine! Follow the path to the left of the fence to where it veers left away from it and carry on down to a track at a large turning area. TURN RIGHT along this rough track to where it veers left to a gate. This is easily passed on the right. Keep following the track and pass by a fenced open pit, a part of Bryn Eglwys Quarry. A path continues from here and descends an old incline and through a gate. Keep following the track to a track junction. IGNORE the one going up to the right and the one going down

WALK 19

to the left. Carry straight on ignoring the first stile and padlocked gate on the left to reach a rustic kissing gate on the left and old finger post.

4 Go through the gate to enter Coed Hendrewallog. Descend gradually at first then more steeply down a flight of steps to a marker post. TURN LEFT acutely and follow the path down, steep in places, to the Nant Gwernol. Follow the path alongside the very pretty stream to a footbridge on the left. IGNORE this although a seat on the right may be utilised for resting! Continue ahead alongside the tumbling stream to arrive above a footbridge. Descend rock steps to this carefully, especially so in the wet, to the bridge. This was crossed earlier in the walk. IGNORE the path going up to the right but return to Abergynolwyn by retracing steps of the outward walk.

*J*ohn **Pugh of Penegoes**, *a village not far from Machynlleth, started quarrying at Bryn Eglwys in 1844. In 1864 it was taken over by the Aberdyfi Slate Company Ltd who built 70 houses in Abergynolwyn. As demand for roofing slate increased some 8,000 tons of these were produced in 1877. However, the cost of producing slate was high and the company became unprofitable. In 1881 the quarry was sold to William McConnell whose family continued operations until 1911when it was sold to Mr (later Sir) Henry Haydn Jones MP. An engine on the Talyllyn Railway is named after him. The quarry closed finally in 1946.*

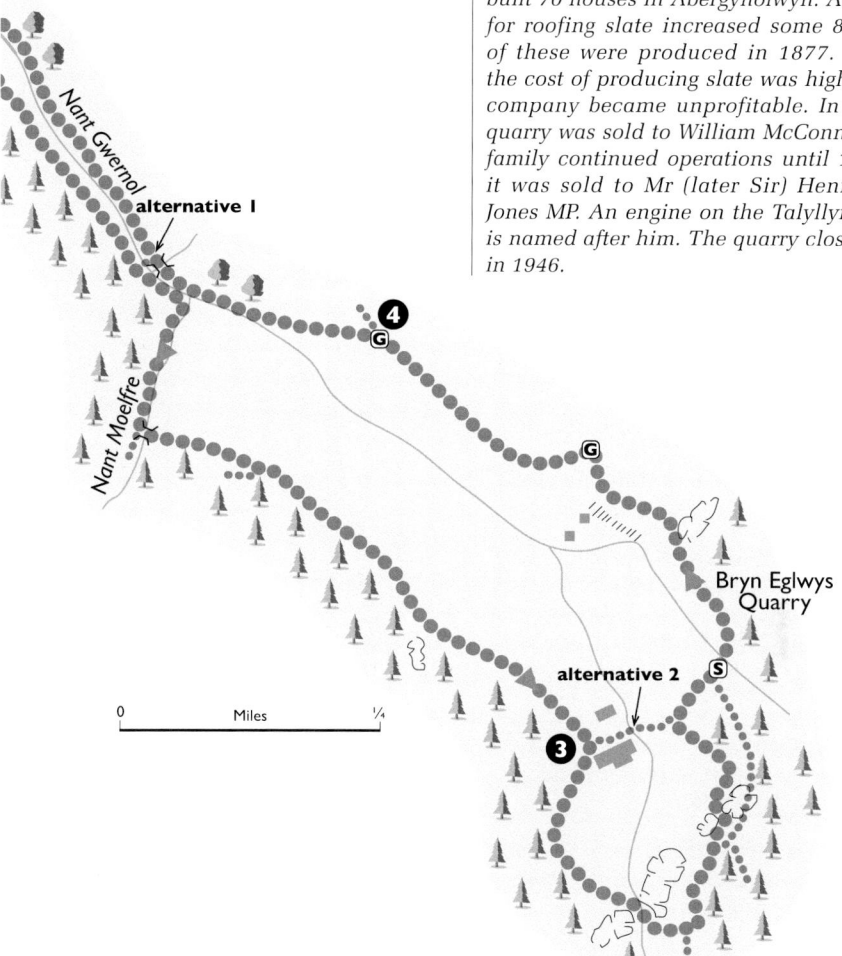

WALK 20
ABERCWMEIDDAW QUARRY

DESCRIPTION This is a much better walk than first appearances would suggest. Although it is only 1½ miles long it is very interesting and includes a view of the 'Corris Binocular'. After passing through some lovely woodland there is an extensive view across the valley to Gaewern Mine. Allow 1½ hours to appreciate this walk.

START Close to a road junction in Upper Corris.

DIRECTIONS Turn off the A487 in Upper Corris either just before the speed restriction signs when coming from the Machynlleth direction or just before the speed de-restriction signs when coming from the north or Dolgellau direction. Follow this road for 200 yards to a 'T' junction. Park opposite this but do not block the gates.

1 Pass to the left of the padlocked double gates and follow the wide track up to where it levels and passes some ruins. Where the track splits follow the track down to the quarry floor. Up to left is a stony slope. This is ascended to reach the 'Corris Binocular'. *It is NOT recommended to climb up into either of the tunnels*. Return to the top of the quarry and the junction.

2 TURN RIGHT and up. Keeping the fence and the tumbling stream to the left continue up the track/path to pass by a stark ruin. Beyond the fence on the left is a pool, a reservoir for the quarry. *DO NOT try and reach this.* Keep following the track to reach a stream. Cross this on stepping stones but not in wet weather! The track rises again and continues to a level section. Carry on to where the track rises again.

3 TURN LEFT on the clearly seen path and descend to and through the gate. *There is a great view of Gaewern Mine across the valley along here.* The path keeps right of the slate/wire fence and continues down to where it becomes a track. This goes down and bears left to a gate at a track junction. Pass through the gate and carry on down to a tarmac road. Follow this back to the car parking area.

*Q**uarrying* started here on what was known as the 'Broad Vein' around 1849 and by 1882 around 188 men worked here and produced 4,173 tons of usable slate. To avoid flooding and also to give access to the mill a 250 yards long tunnel was driven. The right hand tunnel of the 'Corris Binocular' is 30 feet long whilst the left hand one is 280 feet. They were probably bored in the late 1860s by a Brunton wire rope driven disc.

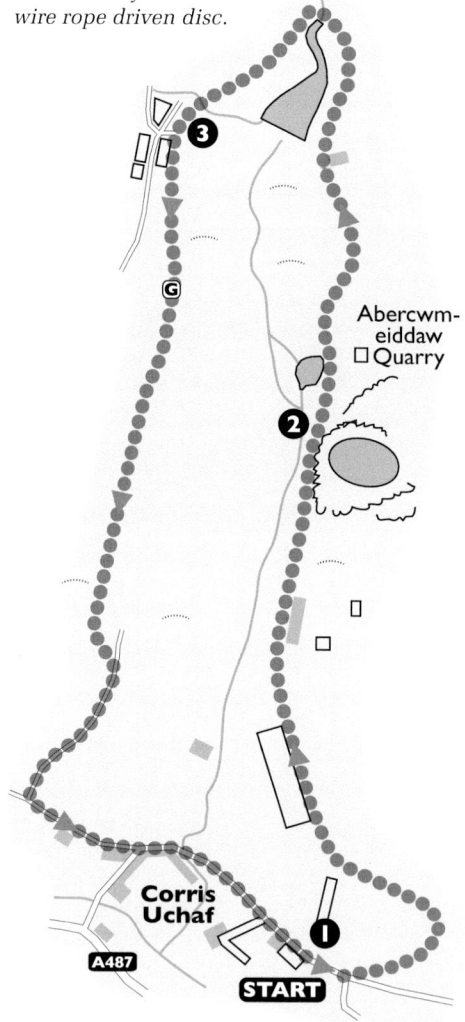

WALKS 20 & 21

WALK 21
ABERLLEFENNI QUARRIES
Incorporating Foel Frochan, Ceunant Ddu & Hen Gloddfa

DESCRIPTION This is an easy 1¼ mile walk easily followed on a good path, track and finally road taking a very casual hour to complete. There are lovely views of the Llefenni Valley and the 'Alma' on Foel Grochan is most impressive.

START At the renovated small quarry office at the far side of Aberllefenni by the information panel and slate slab with a wheel attached indicating the Llwybr yr Olwyn.

DIRECTIONS Turn off the A487 towards Corris by the Braich Goch Inn. Drive down into Corris and continue through the village and along the pretty road to Aberllefenni. Just before entering the village note the fine slate steps that led up to the station. Continue past a row of cottages with the Wincilate slate works opposite. Continue another 100 yards to roadside parking by the information panel close to the renovated building. Be careful not to block access. There is a phone box close by on the opposite side of the road.

There is some evidence that quarrying commenced here in 1500 or thereabouts, perhaps even as early as the 14th century! The slate is found in the Narrow Vein. Slab was mined almost exclusively. It was of exceptional quality and has few joints. The vein dips at 70° to the south east and goes all the way through the hill known as Foel Grochan. The early quarrying was high up the hillside and created the 'Alma'. In 1853 a slab weighing 125 tons was taken. Later quarrying took place underground. In total there were eight levels spaced at 60 feet or so between each other. The lowest (number 8) was at the valley floor. The floor of the 'Alma' is on level 4 and stretches up to level 3.

Wincilate manufacture slate products although some of the finishing takes place at their subsidiary works at Inigo Jones at Groeslon, near Caernarfon.

The slate on the western side of the valley is different in quality to the eastern or Foel Grochan side. The quarries of Ceunant Ddu and Hen Gloddfa have slate that splits easily and produces fine roofing slate. Most of the extraction took place underground. Work ceased in Hen Gloddfa in the 1960s.

Walk up the path to the left of the house and past the sign indicating the Llwybr Hengae Path. Pass through a kissing gate and continue along the obvious path below and between the spoil heaps rising chaotically up to the Hen Gloddfa and Ceunant Ddu Quarries. *There is a great view of the 'Alma' of Foel Grochan across the valley.* The path rises and descends slightly before continuing to a kissing gate. Pass through this to an access track. TURN RIGHT and follow the track to go through a gate to the road going up the valley. TURN RIGHT and follow the road back to the start. *There is a great view of Foel Grochan Quarry up to the left and the extent of Ceunant Ddu and Hen Gloddfa over to the right.*

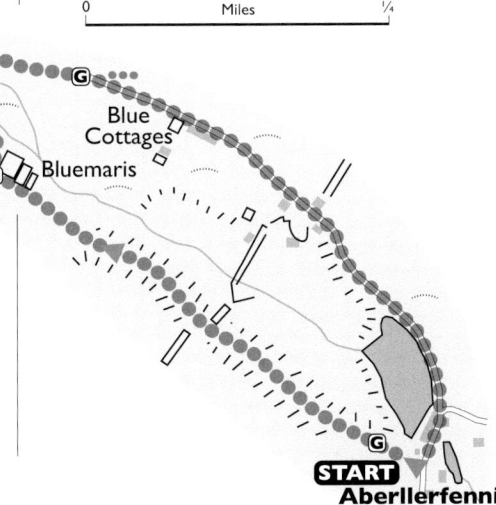

WALK 22
A SLATE MINING VILLAGE & ABERCORRIS QUARRY

DESCRIPTION This 2¼ mile walk explores the village of Corris and follows the access track to the quarry. Part way up the track a remarkable Italianate garden is passed. Although entry into the garden is not allowed a great deal of it can be seen. The walk is easily followed and takes no more than 1½ hours.

START At the Corris Craft Centre. This avoids clogging up the narrow village road with cars.

DIRECTIONS Leave the A487 at the prominent brown signs indicating the turning to the Craft Centre. Coming from the Machynlleth direction this will be a left turn, whilst coming from the north it will be a right turn.

1 TURN LEFT out of the car park and follow the access road out to the A487. There is a bus stop on the right. Cross the road to the bus stop on the far side and TURN RIGHT. Follow the path to where it zig zags down a walled path into Corris arriving opposite the entry to the Corris Railway and Museum. Both of these are well worth a visit. There are toilets on the far side of the road. Corris was once a very thriving community. At the turn of the 19thC there were 14 shops, 4 chapels and a church, 3 banks, 2 schools, 2 pubs, had its own bakery, a weekly newspaper and had a prize winning silver band not to mention successful football, cricket and rugby teams. TURN LEFT and walk through the village passing the institute and a café to the Slaters Arms.

2 TURN LEFT up the road immediately beyond the pub where a sign indicates Corris Hostel is only 200 yards away. The road rises steeply and passes the Adrian Rainsford Centre to reach the hostel which was the old school. *This was built in 1872 in response to the Education Act of 1870. There were 4 classrooms that taught 4 – 11 year olds.* Easier walking continues to a marker and finger post on the right directing the way up the quarry access track. Follow this up quite steeply between walls to the 'Renaissance Italian' garden. *The cottage was built in 1841 but the garden began being built in 1980. Included are the Leaning Tower of Pisa' the 'Rialto Bridge' in Venice, 'Palladio' the most imitated architect in history is well represented. There is no access but most of the miniature replicas can be seen from the track. Of great note here though is a plaque to Wilfred Owen MC. He was born on the 18th March 1893 and died in battle during the 1st World War on 4th November 1918 only a week before the Armistice was signed! Wilfred is regarded as one of the most eminent poets of that war. His poetry vividly portrayed the horrors of war. A few lines etched onto a slab of slate reads:*

> *The pallor of girls' brows shall be their pall;*
> *Their flowers the tenderness of patient minds,*
> *And each slow dusk a drawing down of blinds.*

These are the last three lines from, perhaps, his most poignant poem 'Anthem for Doomed Youth'.

Keep following the track up through conifers to reach a wriggly tin roofed shed. This was the Caban for the quarry. Cabans were where the quarry workers met to have lunch and to rest. Just beyond this is a wall and all that remains of the mill. Continue to a marker post by a tiny stream. A path going off to the right leads to the actual quarry but is not recommended as it loose, steep and overgrown.

3 Cross the stream and follow the path as it bears left and down. There are more ruins in the woodland below. Continue down and through a waymarked gate. Carry on down the grassy path with a great view of Gaewern Mine across the valley on the opposite hillside. Pass below a spoil heap and a finger post to a marker post at the junction with a track. TURN RIGHT down this to go through a waymarked gate to the road.

WALK 22

4 TURN LEFT. Follow the road towards Corris to some houses. TURN RIGHT 50 yards past these through a small gate leading from a parking area. There is a waymark on the fence corner. The path descends through the Nature Reserve to the footbridge over the Afon Deri. Cross this and bear right up to the A487. TURN LEFT down this for 250 yards and TURN LEFT on the obvious path, the old miner's path. Follow this as it continues below road level to reach the A487 once more. Cross the road to return to the Corris Craft Centre car park.

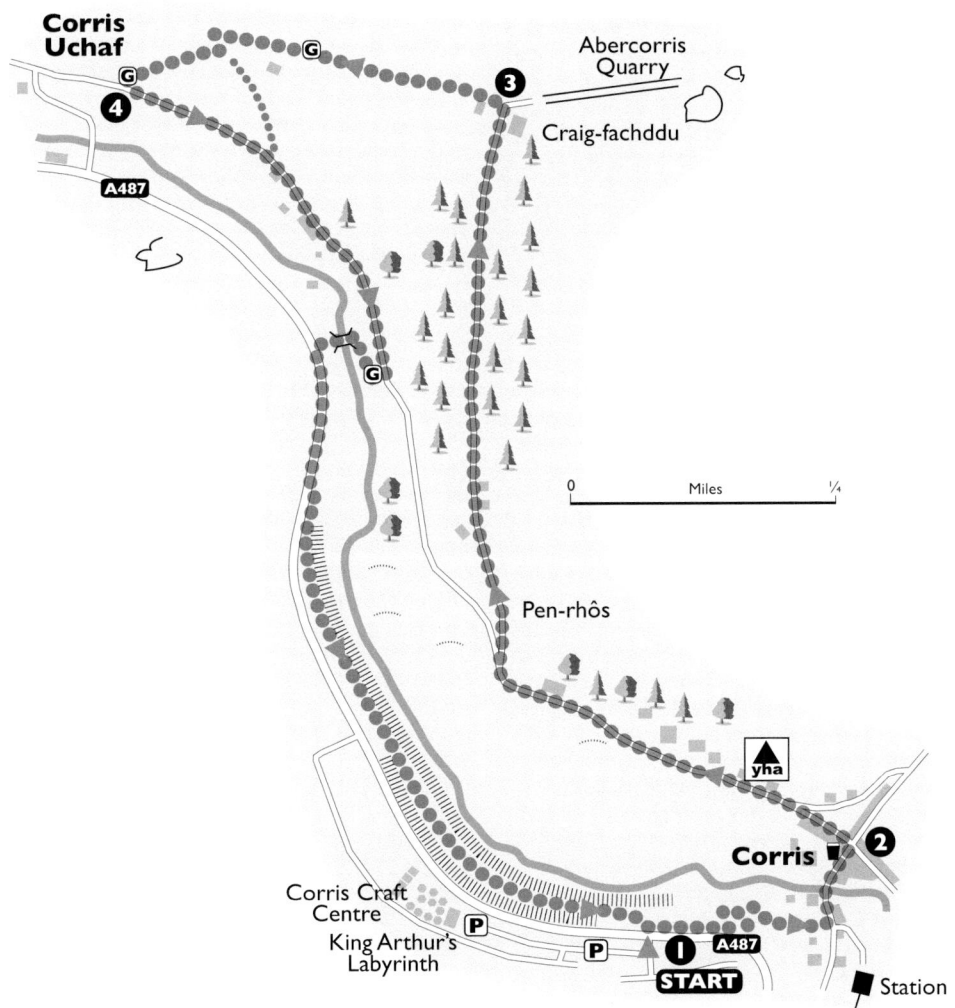

WALK 23
RATGOED

DESCRIPTION This is a pleasant 4½ mile walk exploring the remains of Ratgoed. Situated in a quiet valley scenery varies from lovely woodland and streams at the start to the remote Cwm Ratgoed. There are many ruins hidden amongst the trees in the Cwm. The walk is easily followed and clearly signed. Allow 2¾ hours.

START At the renovated small quarry office at the far side of Aberllefenni by the information panel and slate slab with a wheel attached indicating the Llwybr yr Olwyn.

DIRECTIONS Turn off the A487 towards Corris by the Braich Goch Inn. Drive down into Corris and continue through the village and along the pretty road to Aberllefenni. Just before entering the village note the fine slate steps that led up to the station. Continue past a row of cottages with the Wincilate slate works opposite. Continue another 100 yards to roadside parking by the information panel close to the renovated building. Be careful not to block access. There is a phone box close by on the opposite side of the road.

1 Walk up the road to the junction. TURN RIGHT down the dead end road to where the tarmac ends and a gate in front. DO NOT go through this. Pass to the left of a building then TURN RIGHT at the end of it. Go through three gates in quick succession to cross a footbridge. BEAR LEFT and climb over a waymarked stile. The path continues through a gap in the fence to reach a track. Go up this to the right. Carry on up the fenced track to go through a gate. BEAR LEFT to a gate ahead. DO NOT go through this but follow the fence as it turns 90° to the right. Go up to and over a waymarked stile. There is a ruin to the right. At the path junction 50 yards ahead TURN LEFT. Follow the path with a wall and fence to the left to pass through a waymarked kissing gate. Continue through lovely woodland to go through another waymarked kissing gate.

2 TURN LEFT immediately down a narrow path with a pretty stream tumbling down on the left to the river. Walk upstream to a much clearer path. TURN LEFT through a gate to cross the footbridge. Follow the path to the left and DO NOT go right through the garden of the house. The path leads up to a large layby. TURN RIGHT along the road to the start of a track 150 yards further. TURN LEFT up this and follow it to where it splits at a 'Y' junction with a marker post. Go down to the right and through a gate and the kissing gate 50 yards further left of a padlocked gate. The Nant Ceiswyn is on the left. The track continues to where a white house is seen across the river. *This is Ffynnon Badarn otherwise known as 'Cadbury House'. It was bought by the Cadbury chocolate family in the 1960s. The family were, for the time, kind to their staff allowing them to use the house for holidays. It was also used by the Bourneville family who used it as a base for hill walking. Supposedly there is a well here and Ffynnon Badarn means St Padarn's Well.* Continue to where the track splits at a marker post and 'Y' junction. There are spoil heaps here

3 Go straight ahead on the right arm of the 'Y' to a gate with ruins to the left and right. Continue and pass a fine ruin with an arched doorway and windows 50 yards ahead on the right. *This was the Calvinistic Methodist chapel and opened in 1871.* At the next 'Y' junction go straight ahead to another ruin and pass this to the left. *This was the blacksmith's.* Behind it are the ruins of the slate dressing sheds. To the right are more ruins with the one closest to the track was the weigh bridge. Up to the right is an overgrown incline. Continue past a marker post and through a walled section of old tramway to Ratgoed Hall on the left. *This was owned by the quarry owner Horatio Nelson Hughes a wealthy Liverpudlian. He built the Hall in 1870. In 1940 it became a Youth Hostel.* Pass through the old metal gate to enter more open country. Continue to a large sycamore tree on the left just before the track descends to Dolgoed an old Quaker House. *This is possibly the oldest house in Merionnydd and has been in the hands of the same family since the 1600s.*

WALK 23

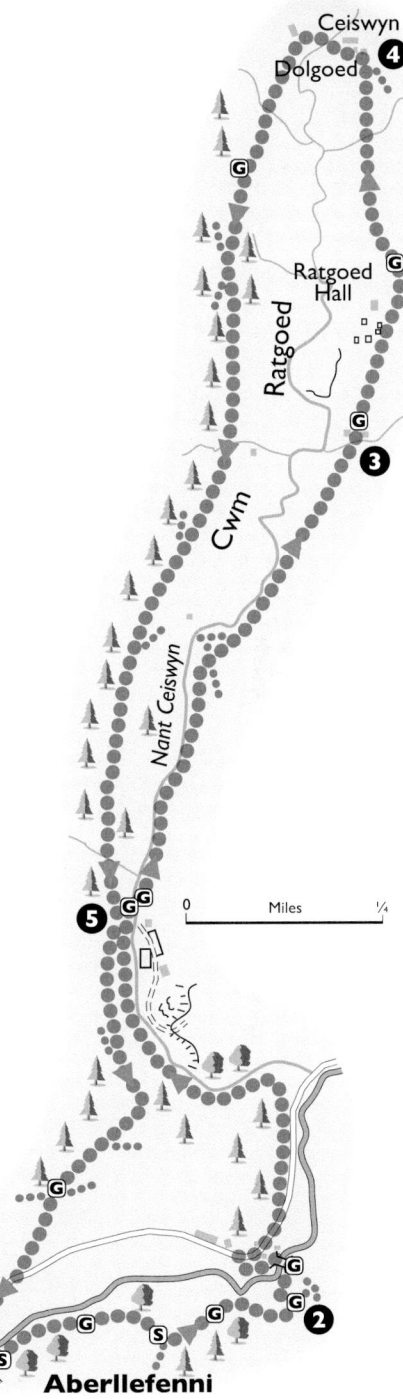

4 TURN LEFT as indicated and cross the field keeping to the left of the solar panels to a waymarked gate. Pass through this and descend a narrow steep path – care – to a tall Scots Pine. BEAR RIGHT to the track and TURN LEFT along it. TURN RIGHT over the waymarked footbridge. Continue and pass through a kissing gate and TURN LEFT to join a track. Ceiswyn Farmhouse is up to the right. *It was built in the 1500s. The Red Brigands of Dinas Mawddwy were an infamous group of brigands, or highwaymen, with predominantly red hair. They were a lawless group and one of their attacks achieving notoriety occurred here. They captured and killed a local judge, Sir Lewis Owain, in a revenge attack for having sentenced some of their group tried and executed. The judge's companion was Sion Lloyd who survived the ambush. Legend tells us that Lloyd hid swords in the chimney in case of another attack!* Follow the track gently up to go through a waymarked kissing gate to enter the forest. Continue through this to go through another waymarked kissing gate. Continue down to the track junction of the outward walk.

5 TURN RIGHT at the finger post and follow the indistinct path across the cleared hillside to join a track. TURN LEFT along this. Go up a short rise to a marker post. BEAR RIGHT and descend a path quite steeply to go through a waymarked gate. Carry on down to where the path becomes a track again and descend to the road at a marker post. TURN RIGHT back to the start of the walk.

***R**atgoed was opened in the mid 19th century. The main workings were on eight levels and worked the Narrow Vein. Output peaked at around 800 tons, but a more common tonnage was around the 1882 figure of 434 from the 35 men workforce. Ratgoed produced mainly slab with items like mantelpiece being the only finished products. The chapel ceased services in 1925 but Sunday school continued until the Second World War after which it closed in 1946 when a re-start was abandoned.*

WALK 24
QUARRY TRAIL AT THE CENTRE FOR ALTERNATIVE TECHNOLOGY

DESCRIPTION Based upon the Llwyngwern Quarry this is a very pleasant 1 mile walk on good paths. There are many information panels and the actual quarry is quite impressive. There are good views and the steep bits are very short. A couple of picnic sites can be utilised if so desired. There is however a small fee for admittance. Allow an hour for the main walk, 45 minutes for the medium and 30 minutes for the short.
START Close to the café.
DIRECTIONS CAT is easily reached from the A487 some 3 miles north of Machynlleth and is served by the T2, X27, 30 and 34 bus services. The Centre is clearly signed from the main road from whatever direction it is approached.

From the café the start is clearly seen and is signed The Quarry Trail. Little in the way of description is needed but a brief one follows. A level start leads to 'Y' junction at point 1 and a right turn leads steeply up and is the steepest part of the walk. Pass The Hairy Hut and descend steeply to the quarry viewpoint. Go up again to point 6. Turn right here for the short route back to the main complex.

Go up to the left to a picnic area at point 9 and the reservoir used by CAT and water for machinery. Continue past the ruin of a weighbridge to point 10 where the medium length walk goes to the right.

Carry on past he fine viewpoint looking across to Tarren y Gesail 2,188 feet and past several information panels. The clearly followed path leads down to the information point and shop at the top of the cliff railway.

After the walk and perhaps a bite to eat in the café it is well worth having a look around at the many exhibits.

Quarrying commenced around 1835 but output never exceeded 1,000 tons. In 1883 around 915 tons were produced from the 35 men who worked there at the time. The quarry closed 1953. The mill area is now used by CAT. Slate was taken down to there from the quarry by an incline which

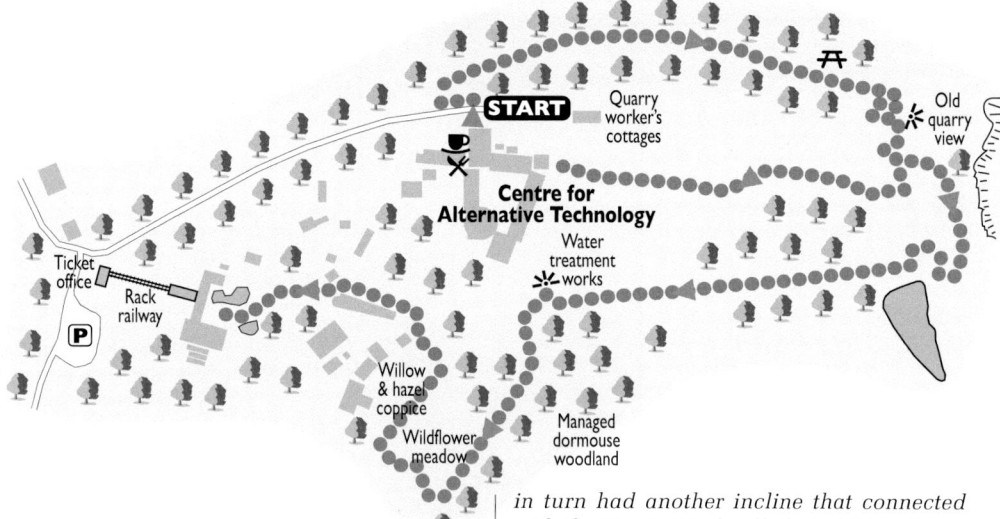

in turn had another incline that connected with the Corris, Machynlleth and River Dovey Tramway in the early 1860s.

WALK 25
RHIWFACHNO, RHIWBACH, BLAEN Y CWM & CWT Y BUGAIL

DESCRIPTION This is a superb, not to be missed, 5 mile walk that ventures into the high land between Cwm Penmachno and Blaenau Ffestiniog. There are some fine ruins and great views, especially down into Cwm Penmachno. The boiler house chimney is spectacular as are the mill ruins. The original quarry is hidden from view being situated in the forest. It is a deep flooded pit over 440 feet deep! Rhiwbach is one of the most remote quarries in Snowdonia. Allow 5 hours which gives plenty of time to explore this fascinating area.

START Roadside parking in Cwm Penmachno.

DIRECTIONS From Betws y Coed follow the A5 towards Llangollen as far as the Conwy Falls Café. Turn right here on to the B4406 and follow it to Penmachno. Drive through the village and turn left at The Eagles pub and bunkhouse at the sign indicating that it is 3 miles to Cwm Penmachno. Continue until reaching spoil heaps on the left just before the final houses seen beyond a 90° right hand bend. There is room here for a number of cars. Up to the left is a gate and kissing gate.

1 Go through the kissing gate. IGNORE the path going off to the right. The track goes up and through the Rhiwfachno Quarry. Go past a wall and then left across a level area to where the track rises steadily in stages to pass to the right of a prominent incline, ignoring the more obvious track going to the left. This is the new track! *Over to the right is a clean quarried area of slate with prominent strata. The dip of the slate is 47 ½ degrees and this area became known locally as Hill 60. So named after two local men who were killed in the First World War! Over to the left there is a fine arched tunnel passing through the incline.* Continue up to re-join the new track. Continue up this for 150 yards then TURN RIGHT up the obvious path. This quickly turns into a track. This is the old quarry track and continues up to re-join the new track once again. Turn right up this and continue quite steeply to a ladder stile.

2 Climb over this to where the gradient eases. Follow the track up past a breached dam, seen down to the left, to a stile to the left of a gate. It is easier to go through the gate to enter conifers. At the end of these cross a bridge of old railway lines and go up a short rise. *Over to the left the old Rhiwbach village is seen, with a narrow path heading off towards it.* Continue up to a 'Y' junction. Follow the right arm towards a fence guarding a deep pit. This was known locally as Cwm End Note also the heavily fortified entrance down to the right. This is the exit to the mine along with another over to the left that is used by modern day explorers. There are companies that take guided trips through here. Cross the stile and descend, carefully, to the floor. Return to where the path goes off to Rhiwbach village. Follow this path, through sedges, to the village. This was once the 'main' road into the village as can be determined by the upright slate slabs marking the edge of that road. *Rhiwbach was one of the most remote quarries in the industry. Frequently cut off during bad weather a village was built that encompassed family quarters as well as barracks for single men, a shop, chapel and school house.*

3 Continue past the village, having explored it, to a prominent finger stone. Go to the right up the shallow incline to the left of a spoil heap to a level area at the top of it. *Note how ruinous the area is hereabouts.* TURN RIGHT for 50 yards to where an easy short climb up, but take care, leads to the top of the spoil heap. *There are superb views of the village from here to the right whilst down to the left is the ruin of the 'New Mill'.* Continue along through more ruins to reach a track and a fine chimney stack. To the right of the chimney stack is a ladder stile and climb over it. Follow the faint narrow path up on the right of the incline to join it. Continue up it to the top. *There are the remains of the sheave housing and brake-*

man's hut here at the start of the Rhiwbach Tramway. The view down to the chimney and ruins is spectacular.

4 Continue along the track that was once the Rhiwbach Tramway past a pit and chamber down on the left. This is the start of Blaen y Cwm Quarry. At the junction IGNORE the track going up to the left. Carry straight on avoiding deep puddles where necessary! The small but main part of Blaen y Cwm quarry is down to the right. At the rock cutting a path up to the right avoids the deeper water to re-join the tramway. *Snowdon 3,560 feet, Crib y Ddysgl 3,494 feet and the Crib Goch Ridge come into view here. The mountain straight ahead is Moel Penamnen 2,034 feet.* Keep following the track as it bends to the right to reach the ruins at Cwt y Bugail.

5 Follow the obvious incline going up from the ruins. *Part way up here Moelwyn Bach 2,329 feet, Craigysgafn 2,260 feet and Moelwyn Mawr 2,562 feet come into view.* The incline levels at more ruins and continues as a tramway through a cutting to reach the Cwt y Bugail quarry along with the dramatic entrance into the underground workings. *Note the fine slate wall on the right.* A short tunnel on the left leads into a smaller quarry. Two levels can be seen at the far side. Return to the main ruins down the incline. Two options avail themselves from here: **1**, return the same way back to Cwm Penmachno as the outward walk. **This is recommended.** Or **2**, it is possible to make a circular walk from the ruins but the way is pathless until reaching the Rhwibach drainage tunnel. It is also boggy with many sedges and tussock grass mixed with heather. Route finding will be difficult in mist! The only advantage is that it passes the drainage tunnel of Rhiwbach Mine and has a great view of Rhiwfachno Quarry near the end of the walk. The following is a description for those who want a circular walk.

6 TURN LEFT just before the incline levels at the bottom on a narrow path across the level top of a spoil heap. Just before the end descend easily to the left on the path.

A faint path is followed but this quickly fades. Continue around the hillside and cross a deep grass and sedge filled gully at the low point of it. Keep contouring to where the hillside starts to descend. Bear very slightly right to an outcrop of quartz rock. Continue down to reach a fence and stile. Cross the stile. *There is a wonderful view of Cwm Penmachno from here.* (Note: if you arrive at the fence and there is no stile TURN RIGHT and follow it to either reach the stile or a ladder stile further along next to the forest. Climb over this and follow the forest edge with the fence to the right down to a stile on the right).

7 TURN RIGHT and, veering gradually away from the fence, descend to another stile. Climb over this to enter the forest. Walk straight down through this to reach the exit of the drainage tunnel for Rhiwbach Mine. This is now the way in for people exploring the mine. TURN RIGHT along the very clear and damp path taking care on the many tree roots sticking up. Continue through the forest to climb over a stile where the forest ends. TURN LEFT and continue down the path to a ruined drum house at the top of a short but fine incline. *There is a very fine view of Rhiwfachno Quarry from here.* Descend the incline and follow the path down to the kissing gate passed through at the start of the walk to the car parking area.

Rhiwfachno Quarry *started being worked in 1818, and ceased in 1962. There were*

WALK 25

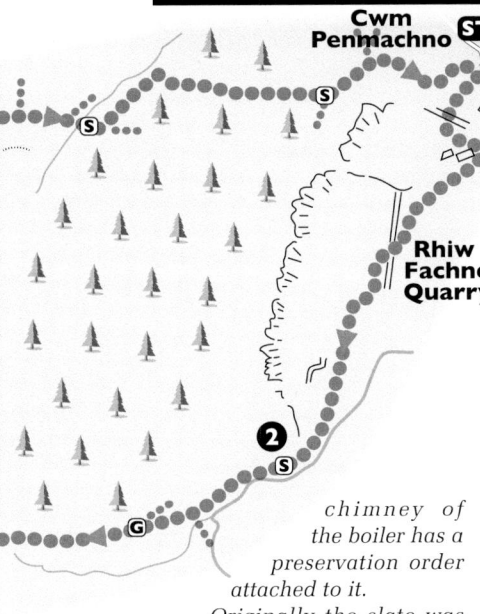

three mills but the area where they were has been landscaped with two small buildings and a part of a mill the only remnants. The fine crenulated wall was demolished and much of the tips used to fill in the pit. The most obvious feature is the fine table incline. This brought block down to the mills from the upper workings whilst rubbish was up hauled. The quarry provided work for at least 100 men until the onset of World War II. It closed because of the lack of skilled manpower. Slate was initially carted to Trefriw wharf then later to Betws y Coed station. These days it is hard to imagine boats coming up the Afon Conwy as far as Trefriw!

*R*hiwbach quarry and Blaen-y-cwm quarry were very different to other quarries in the slate industry in one important aspect. To get the finished product out it had to go upwards! Because of this an engine house had to be built that would power the incline from the bottom with the wire rope passing around a sheave at the top. The engine house also provided power for the machinery and the underground inclines. Work started at the beginning of the 19th century and seriously developed in 1840s. Initially works were somewhat south of what became the main complex. This area developed into a deep pit and is now flooded. It was worked out by the 1880s and work transferred to the present site. The pit working here, started in the 1860s, was later developed extensively underground to encompass eight levels. Output peaked in 1869 at over 8,000 tons. By 1890 the 81 men employed here produced only 2,260 tons. In 1935 tonnage was down to 1,000 and final closure came in 1952 due to manning problems. The chimney of the boiler has a preservation order attached to it.

Originally the slate was carried down to Cwm Machno and thence to Trefriw but from the 1830s it was carted down Cwm Teigl to Maentwrog for shipping down the Afon Dwyryd. This continued until the opening of the Rhiwbach Tramway in 1863. Slate was carried on this past Cwt-y-bugail, Llyn Bowydd, Llyn Newydd to the head of three inclines leading down to Blaenau Ffestiniog. It was then transported on the Ffestiniog Railway to the newly opened wharf at Porthmadog and continued to do so until closure.

Blaen y Cwm Quarry started life somewhere between 1813 and 1818 until final closure in 1914. The greatest period of development came in the 1870s when the mill was built. There were many workings but output was small.

Cwt y Bugail (The Shepherd's Hut). This is the original quarry of that name although it has now been given to Manod Quarry. Starting life in the 1820' large scale development took place in the 1860s after the Rhiwbach Tramway was built. In the 1870s output peaked at 3,500 tons per year when 116 men worked there. The quarrymen lived in barracks due to the remoteness of the site. Closure came in the 1960s when the tramway was used for the last time

WALK 26

MINLLYN

DESCRIPTION This is a straightforward, easily followed 1¼ miles linear walk which is steep up and steep down. That said the remains are good and the quarry pit is impressive with a stream tumbling down the vertical face. There are good views of the Dyfi valley from the top of the incline whilst the conifers are tall and impressive. A fine arched tunnel is one of the main features. Allow 1¼ hours if exploring the arched tunnel.

START At the layby on the forest track at start of the path.

DIRECTIONS Turn off the A470 in Dinas Mawddwy at signs for Ty Derw by the war memorial. Turn right in front of the sign indicating 1 – 3 Godre'r Coed and go up to a 'T' junction. Turn right and drive up the track for 300 yards to laybys, one on the left and another to the right at the start of the path on the left.

Follow the clearly seen path through the undergrowth. The path steepens and passes through some fine, very tall conifers to where the path levels at a waymarked stile. Climb over this to the ruins. Continue to the fine arched tunnel at the foot of two inclines. For those who do not mind getting their feet wet it is possible to pass through this to the floor of the main pit. The main entrance to the mine is easily spotted. *DO NOT ENTER as there is deep water in places and long drops as well as route finding being quite complicated.* Go up the shallow incline to the right to the top of the pit. Take CARE here. Note the stream tumbling down. TURN LEFT to the steep incline and follow it up to the top for a fine view of the ruins and the surrounding hills. Return down the steep incline to the ruins and then back to the layby.

Minllyn *was worked from the early 19thC. Underground development started to take place in the 1840s. Around 140 men were employed but production was low and did not warrant that many workers. A mill was built on site and processed the slate. It had three saws, three dressers and possibly a similar number of planning machines. These last pre-dated anything at Blaenau Ffestiniog. This slate was sent down an incline to the valley. Later a much larger mill was built there and processed slate from Minllyn as well as other scratchings in the area. It reputedly had 40 machines – a mixture of saw and dressers, but apparently, no planers. The finished products were sent via a short tramway to the rail terminus at Dinas Mawddwy. Interestingly all the tramways were half standard gauge – 2 feet 4¼ inches. The mine closed in 1925. The mill has been renovated and now houses the Meirion Mill shop and café.*

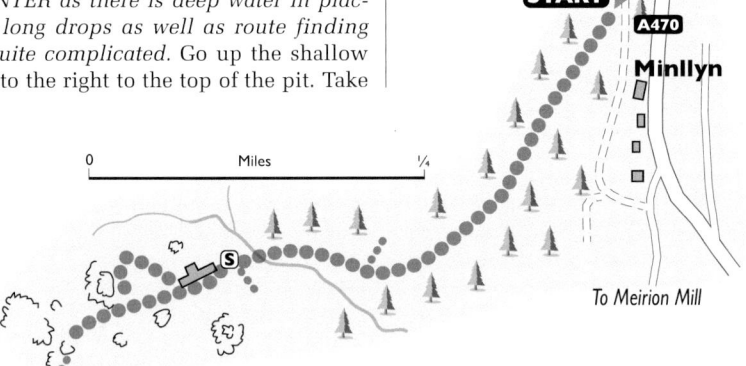

TOURIST MINES AND OTHER SLATE BASED ATTRACTIONS

NATIONAL SLATE MUSEUM
Situated on the outskirts of Llanberis close to Llyn Padarn this tells the story about a way of life. Not only is it the best place for experiencing life as it was during the slate mining days it also gives an insight into the rigours of extracting and fashioning the slate. There are regular demonstrations on how slates are split. There is operational machinery and the 15.4 metres high water wheel is the largest on the British mainland. The experience is free other than the Council operated car park. A whole day could be spent here looking at the exhibits and exploring one or more of the slate paths described earlier. For more information look at the web site: www.nationalslatemuseum.ac.uk or telephone 0300 111 2 333

When visiting the following show mines please be aware that the temperature inside is well below that outside in summer. It is between 8 to 10 degrees C (around 50 degrees F). As such it is advisable to wear warm clothing. Wear shoes or boots having a good grip as the ground can be slippery.

LLECHWEDD SLATE CAVERNS
This is situated on the outskirts of Blaenau Ffestiniog some ¾ mile north of the town. There are many attractions here not least is the story of the Llechwedd Caverns in the interpretive centre. This also shows how slate was extracted and processed. There is also a reconstructed village showing how the miners lived. Access to the underground workings is by a funicular railway. Descending over 500 feet it is the steepest passenger railway in Britain. The tour involves visiting 10 huge chambers and ½ mile of tunnels to arrive at a very beautiful underground lake. In fact the mine has over 25 miles of tunnels. Other attractions here include mountain biking, zip lines and a huge underground trampoline. For more information look at the web site: www.llechwedd-slate-caverns.co.uk or telephone 01766 830306.

Llechwedd was first mined in 1848 and slate production was greatly improved by new technologies such as slate cutting saws in 1851. In the 1920's electricity was introduced which powered the underground railway systems. John Greaves was the owner of Llechwedd as well as several others in the area and he was much involved with the Ffestiniog Railway. This enabled slate products being transported to a private quay in Porthmadog before being shipped to the four corners of the world. Germany had a great demand for Llechwedd slate products.

There are other developments here – Bounce Below, Zip World Titan and Antur Stiniog. This last is a not for profit organisation set up in 2007 with a view 'to develop the potential of the Outdoor Sector in the Ffestiniog area in a sustainable and innovative way for the benefit of the local residents and economy'. They have developed a series of exciting mountain bike trails in the area and are aiming to develop the disused railway line between Blaenau Ffestiniog and Trawsfynydd. A unique, to the UK, Velorail project is also planned along this. The concept uses low carbon, sustainable bicycle technology to propel an adapted carriage along the disused railway line. This would make it attractive to families.

LLANFAIR SLATE CAVERNS
Although smaller than Llechwedd Caverns it is no less impressive. Situated not far from Harlech on the A496 coast road the mine is entered down Jacobs Ladder and you are free to explore. On emerging there is a breath-taking view of Cardigan Bay, stretching all the way from the Preseli Mountains in Carmarthenshire to the Llyn Peninsula, whilst closer to is Shell

Island. For more information look at the web site: www.llanfairslatecaverns.co.uk or telephone 01766 780247.

Slate was mined here between 1890 and 1910. Here there it is possible to explore the caverns by yourself. Some of the scenes of the 1995 film 'First Knight' were filmed here.

KING ARTHUR'S LABYRINTH

A part of Corris Craft Centre, close to Machynlleth, this show mine is explored by boat and foot. Themed on King Arthur it is best described as an underground storytelling adventure. A mysterious hooded boatman takes you through a magical waterfall into the world of King Arthur and the Dark Ages. Once the boat is docked the 'hooded' boatman guides you through vast caverns and tunnels telling stories about those times as well as some Welsh legends. Light and sound bring these to life. The Labyrinth is part of the Braich Goch Mine and is on level 6. For more information look at the web site: www.kingarthurslabyrinth.co.uk or telephone 01654 761584. Note that during winter months staff are often not present so delays in returning calls may be experienced.

Next to the Labyrinth there is a Stone Circle. A twisting path in the maze hides eight mythical stories with some very interesting characters. Find all the clues and you win a prize!

CORRIS MINE EXPLORERS

For the adventurous Corris Mine Explorers gives people a chance to explore the ancient working of Braich Goch Mine. Although there are seven levels the exploration covers just three of these, levels 4, 5 and 6. There are three trips available: Taster, a 2 hour Mine Explorer and a ½ day (4 hours) Mine Expedition. Further information and bookings can be made at www.corrismineexplorers.co.uk or telephone 01654 761244.

Slate quarrying at Corris dates back to the 14th century when the Foel Grochan quarry above Aberllefenni was first mined The Braich Goch and Gaewern mines began around 1812 with Gaewern being the first of the two to be worked with Braich Goch itself starting in 1836. In 1848 working at Gaewern ceased and re-started in 1853. During its heyday some 250 men worked in the mine in 1878 and around 7,000 tons of slab and roofing slates were mined. Rising costs and demand saw the mine company collapse in 1906, although six companies continued work until 1970 when the mine finally closed.

ELECTRIC MOUNTAIN

Visiting the vast underground tunnels and chambers of this underground power station is an amazing experience. But why build one here? In the 1950s a pumped storage scheme was undertaken at Blaenau Ffestiniog and was highly successful. As such another scheme was planned. The ideal situation was found on Elidir Fawr. Marchlyn Mawr a small lake below the summit and in the valley Llyn Peris. The huge rambling scar of the Dinorwig quarries provided the ideal place in which to build tunnels to house the power station It took 10 years to build, as well as enlarging the lakes, and was opened by Prince Charles in 1984. Further information can be obtained at www.electricmountain.co.uk or telephone 01286 870636.

Quarrying first took place in 1787. Production increased after 1824 to the extent that around 100,000 tons of slate was produced. Bear in mind that for every 10 tons of rock quarried only 1 ton was usable! At its peak in the late 19th century over 3,000 men worked there making it the largest opencast slate producer in the country. By 1930 the workforce had shrunk to 2,000 and in 1969 production ceased. The slate vein is almost vertical. As such it was worked in stepped galleries.

INIGO JONES SLATE WORKS

Initially the works were established in 1861 to prefabricate school writing slates. Nowadays, self-guided tours of the works give an opportunity to have a go at calligraphy and engraving a piece of slate that you get to keep as a souvenir. There is a large showroom where its slate products are available for purchase as are other Welsh and Celtic gifts. Tours were introduced in the early 1980's by popular demand and commences with a video presentation followed by wandering through the workshops accompanied with a personal taped commentary. There is also a café opening at 10.00 to 17.00. The site is open every day of the year excepting for Christmas and Boxing Days and New Year's Day from 09.00 to 17.00 with a last tour at 16.00. Dogs are welcome. More information can be obtained at www.inigojones.co.uk or calling 01286 830242.

ZIP WORLD

Opened in March 2013 ZIP WORLD VELOCITY in Bethesda quickly achieved international fame. There is a pair of zip lines each a mile long where it is possible to achieve speeds of 100 mph! The wires are 500 feet above the ground making the experience the nearest thing to human flight. The Adventure Terminal provides stunning views of Velocity, Penrhyn Quarry and the lake. Further information can be obtained at www.zipworld.co.uk or telephone 01248 601444.

GO BELOW

For some great underground adventures and challenges this company has a big selection of trips from 5 hours to all day. The mines they explore are some of the longest and deepest in Snowdonia. Mines such as Cwmorthin above Tanygrisiau and Rhiwbach in Cwm Penmachno have a variety of trips. They have bases in Tanygrisiau close to Blaenau Ffestiniog and at Conwy Falls near to Betws y Coed. Further information and bookings can be made at www.go-below.co.uk or telephone 01690 710108.

CENTRE FOR ALTERNATIVE TECHNOLOGY (CAT)

This is situated in the old quarry of Llyngwern just off the A487 some 3 miles north of Machynlleth. There is much to discover here regarding living a greener life from what can be done to your home, how Britain can become Zero Carbon, Green Bookshop, the water balance cliff railway, information on renewable energy, mole hole and quarry trail. There is also a café. Further information can be found at www.cat.org.uk or telephone 01654 705950 or email visit@cat.org.uk

THE NARROW GAUGE RAILWAYS

These were built to facilitate the transportation of slate to the various harbours. For example the Blaenau Ffestiniog slate quarries shipped their slate from Porthmadog, The Dinorwig quarries shipped their slate from Port Dinorwig. The slate mines and quarries at Aberllefenni and Corris shipped their slate to Derwenlas just beyond Machynlleth for shipment. Bryn Eglwys quarry at Abergynolwyn transported their slate to Tywyn on the Talyllyn Railway. All these railways have been preserved by enthusiasts and provide a most memorable experience. The ones pertaining to this book are:

Ffestiniog Railway and Welsh Highland Railway: www.festrail.co.uk or telephone 01766 516024

Llanberis Lake Railway: www.lake-railway.co.uk or telephone 01286 870549

Talyllyn Railway: www.talyllyn.co.uk or telephone (main office) 01654 710472

Corris Railway: www.corris.co.uk or telephone 01654 761303

Penrhyn Quarry Railway: www.penrhynrail.co.uk

Fairbourne Miniature Railway: www.fairbournerailway.com or telephone 01341 250362

Bala Lake Railway: www.bala-lake-railway.co.uk or telephone 01678 540666

Welsh Highland Heritage Railway: www.whr.co.uk or telephone 01766 513402

There are no walks associated with Bala Lake Railway or the Welsh Highland Heritage Railway but they are included as they are within the Snowdonia National Park boundary.

A SELECTION OF FURTHER READING

Snowdonia Slate Trail by Aled Owen ISBN 978-1-898481-80-5

Gazeteer of Slate Quarrying In Wales by Alun John Richards. ISBN 1 84524 074X

Slate Quarrying in Wales by Alun John Richards. ISBN 1 84527 026 6

Cwmorthin Slate Quarry by Graham Isherwood ISBN 0 9522979 1 4

Rhiwbach Slate Quarry by Griff R Jones ISBN 0 9533692 2 6

Welsh Slate by David Gwyn ISBN 978 1 871184 51 8

Dinorwic – The Llanberis Slate Quarry by Reg Chambers Jones ISBN 978 184494 033 2

Slate From Abergynolwyn by Alan Holme, a member of the Talyllyn Preservation Society ISBN 978 0 9565652 4 2

Bryn Eglwys Slate Quarry by Alan Holmes and Sara Eade ISBN 978 0 9565652 4 2

Rhosydd Quarry by M J T Lewis ISBN 078 1 9998134 2 0

Rhosydd – A personal view by Jean Napier ISBN 0 86381 470 0

The Slate Railways Of Wales by Alun John Richards ISBN 0 86381 689 4

Welsh Slate Craft by Alun John Richards ISBN 1 84527 029 0

Slate Quarrying In Corris by Alun John Richards ISBN 1 84524 068 5

Within These Hills – A study of Corris Uchaf by Sara Eade ISBN 978 0 9565652 1 1

The North Wales Quarrymen 1874 – 1922 by R Merfyn Jones ISBN 978 1 78316 175 1

SOME SLATE MINING AND QUARRYING TERMINOLOGY

Adit	The entrance to a mine tunnel from the surface
Balanced incline	An incline with two railway tracks where the descent of the loaded wagons brought up the empty ones
Barracks	The accommodation area used by quarrymen usually through the week but occasionally all year
Black Powder	The original explosive used prior to dynamite
Block	A large piece of quarried slate
Blondin	A wire rope, supported by wooden towers, where a system of pulleys would raise, move and lower rock
Caban	A small shelter built from the waste rock by the miners, normally used as a place of rest and at lunchtimes
Chain incline	A suspended incline using a wire rope instead of a railway line and inclined plane
Chamber	An underground working area that is up to 70 feet wide
Chwarel	Welsh for quarry
Cowjian	A plug chisel that is used for splitting blocks
Cup-boarding	This is the very dangerous practise of cutting into roofing pillars in order to get cheap or free slate
Cyfell	A long wide knife used to trim roofing slates to size
Drum	A horizontal drum around which the wire rope of a balanced incline was wound. Often made from wood
Fire-setting	A very old mining method used to weaken the slate by building a fire against a working face and then quenching with water. Going back almost 2,000 years it was described by Pliny the Elder in 77 AD
Floor	The working level of a quarry or mine and usually numbered
Jwmpah	A long weighted rod weighted close to an end used for manually boring a holeLong weighted rod used to manually bore a hole. Used before the advent of compressed air drills
Launder	A trough used for conveying water to a water wheel
Leat	An artificial watercourse or aqueduct dug into the ground, especially one supplying water to a mill
Level	Horizontal tunnel driven for access or drainage
Mill	The building where slate is reduced by using machinery. At first water was used, then latterly by electricity
Mine	An underground excavation made to extract the slate. Quarry, pit and opencast are used for workings open to daylight

Pillar	A column of slate left to support the roof above
Pillar robbing	Same as cup-boarding
Plug & feathers	A tool that consisted of two half round, tapered, short bars and a wedge. The two bars are inserted into a pre-drilled hole and then the wedge is hammered down between them, splitting the rock. Along with fire-setting, this was a common method of driving a level before the introduction of gunpowder
Pric Mesur	A serrated stick with nail in the end that was used to mark out roofing slate sizes
Quarry	The distinction, in law, between a quarry and mine is somewhat blurred. The term quarry implies that the workings are open to the sky
Rhys	A large mallet used to break up large slate blocks
Rubbish	The waste rock from the mining or quarrying process. It took around 10 tons of rock to produce 1 ton of usable slate
Shot hole	The hole bored into the slate for the insertion of gunpowder
Strike	A tunnel bored horizontally into the slate vein
Terrace	A working level of an open quarry. These, like levels, were numbered
Un-topping	The term used for removing the arth and rock from above the underground workings to remove pillars to gain cheap slate
Twll	A surface pit working
Waliau	Open fronted sheds where slate was hand trimmed and dressed
Water balance	A type of incline where the weight of water was used to raise wagons.
Winding or Drum house	This was built to support the winding mechanism at the head of an incline.

The summit of Pen y Cilgwyn (Mynydd y Cilgwyn) looking towards Anglesey. This is Walk 13..

The main incline in Rhiwfachno quarry with the tops of the launder pillars showing when viewed from the main track through the quarry. This is walk 25.

PRONUNCIATION

Welsh	English equivalent
c	always hard, as in **c**at
ch	as in the Scottish word lo**ch**
dd	as th in **th**en
f	as f in o**f**
ff	as ff in o**ff**
g	always hard as in **g**ot
ll	no real equivalent. It is like 'th' in then, but with an 'L' sound added to it, giving 'thlan' for the pronunciation of the Welsh 'Llan'.

In Welsh the accent usually falls on the last-but-one syllable of a word.

THE COUNTRYSIDE CODE

- Be safe – plan ahead and follow any signs
- Leave gates and property as you find them
- Protect plants and animals, and take your litter home
- Keep dogs under close control
- Consider other people

OPEN ACCESS

Some routes cross areas of land where walkers have the legal right of access under The CRoW Act 2000 introduced in May 2005. Access can be subject to restrictions and closure for land management or safety reasons for up to 28 days a year. Details from: www.naturalresourceswales.gov.uk. Please respect any notices.

About the author,

Des Marshall has had a lifelong interest in mountaineering, climbing, walking, canyoning and caving. As well as being an advisor, trainer and assessor in outdoor activities, he has undertaken many expeditions worldwide but now focuses more on local excursions. After moving away a couple of years ago, the lure of the plethora of exciting walking and climbing became too much and he now lives in Pwhelli on the Llŷn peninsula.

Published by **Kittiwake Books Limited**
3 Glantwymyn Village Workshops, Glantwymyn, Machynlleth, Montgomeryshire SY20 8LY

© Text, map research & photos: Des Marshall 2018

© Maps: Kittiwake Books Ltd 2018

Cover photos: Des Marshall 2018

Care has been taken to be accurate. However neither the author nor the publisher can accept responsibility for any errors which may appear, or their consequences. If you are in any doubt about access, check before you proceed.

Printed by Mixam UK

ISBN: **978 1 908748 54 6**